THE WARRIOR METHOD

The Warrior Method

A PROGRAM

FOR REARING HEALTHY

BLACK BOYS

Raymond A. Winbush, Ph.D.

 Amistad   *An Imprint of* HarperCollins*Publishers*

HarperCollins books may be purchased for educational, business, or sales promotional use. For information, please write: Special Markets Department, HarperCollins Publishers Inc., 10 East 53rd Street, New York, NY 10022.

FIRST EDITION

Designed by Kate Nichols

Printed on acid-free paper

Library of Congress Cataloging-in-Publication Data

Winbush, Raymond A. (Raymond Arnold).
    The warrior method : a program for rearing healthy Black boys / Raymond A. Winbush.—1st ed.
        p.   cm.
    Includes bibliographical references and index.
    ISBN 0-380-97507-6 (acid-free paper)
    1. African American boys—Social conditions.   2. African American teenage boys—Social conditions.   3. African American boys—Conduct of life.   4. African American teenage boys—Conduct of life.   5. Child rearing—United States—Handbooks, manuals, etc.   6. Child rearing—Africa, West.   7. Poro (Society).   I. Title.

E185.86 .W556   2001
649'.15796073—dc21

                                                              2001022335

01   02   03   04   05   10   9   8   7   6   5   4   3   2   1

*To the Winbush men in my life who have made a
difference:*

*Dad, who is with the ancestors
Faraji, my youngest son who has taught me so much
about being a father
Omari, my oldest son whose gentle spirit has been
my teacher
Ron, my brother and best friend
Nicolas, my nephew who has unbounded energy in
all that he does
Windy, my brother who is with Dad*

*To all of you, living and dead, this book is for you
and the love you give me . . .*

Acknowledgments

Writing a book about black boys poses challenges at several levels. Convincing publishers that black boys are important and have their own voice, editors that black boys have a story to tell and a public that is largely afraid to listen to them are not easy tasks.

The Warrior Method could not have been possible without the gentle hand of Carol Taylor guiding it to completion. The ancient and sacred balance between black men and black women is expressed perfectly in the book. She is not only an extraordinarily gifted editor, but she understands what being African in America is all about. My literary agent Heidi von Schreiner also deserves much credit for convincing Avon to publish *The Warrior Method* in the first place.

Manie Barron of HarperCollins was my final editor who taught me a lot about the politics of the publishing industry. He is a solid brother who is willing to take chances with black authors.

Fisk University has been supportive in allowing me to have the time to write as well. Its generous role in providing its faculty and students with many opportunities to examine black life is a tradition I am proud to be a part of. Nikki Giovanni, John Hope Franklin, James Weldon Johnson, Judith Jamison, and its "patron saint" W. E. B. Du Bois, grace its halls and continue to inspire teachers and students to understand the rich traditions, history, and culture of Africans throughout the world.

No author writes in a vacuum. The persons who've most influenced my way of thinking are Frances Cress Welsing, Neely Fuller, Marimba Ani, Molefi Asante, Derrick Bell, Ida B. Wells-Barnett and W. E. B. Du Bois. I share their African-centered worldviews and hopefully have done them justice in talking about race, racism, and black males.

Henri Brooks, chair of the State of Tennessee Black Legislative Caucus; Richard Manson, my attorney and friend, who speaks with an African voice; the Amistad Research Center at Tulane University; Fisk's eminent librarian Jessie Carney Smith; Yaa Asantewa Nzingha, a true African-centered educator; my uncle Herbert Campbell; Lorna Gonsalves-Pinto, whose unwavering opposition to white supremacy inspires me; Jennifer Williams gave me much needed spiritual advice; Asiba Tupahache, whose analysis of victimization is nothing short of brilliant; my brother Ron; Anne and Pat, the mothers of my children; daughter Sharifa; my two sons Omari and Faraji; spirit son Jawanza; Grace Bansa of the *Encyclopaedia Africana* in Accra, Ghana; Jackie Jones; Sam Pieh; Archbishop Emeritus Desmond Tutu and his daughter Naomi; Trudy Moore; Theeda Murphy; Angela Clark; Jerry Laster; and Randall Robinson have all been both direct and indirect influences for the ideas in *The Warrior Method*.

Finally, my mother and father, Dorothy and Harold

Winbush, always taught their sons and daughters to "tell the truth no matter what the price." I wish I could say that I've done that all of the time, but I haven't. This book, however, reflects the truth-telling honesty they encouraged in their children, Harold Jr., Myrna, LaVonne, Raymond, and Ronald. Ultimately, the challenges faced by black boys are challenges faced by all black people. The unpopular truths contained in these pages will be rejected, consciously or unconsciously, by those persons who dismiss the continuing influence of racism in America, and accepted by those who, regardless of color, wish to confront the problems faced by black people in this country.

Contents

Foreword   xv

Prologue   1

Introduction   5
A National Crisis? • Destructive Black Male Behavior •
Constructive Black Male Behavior • The Poro and Sande
Societies • My Own Story

1: The Image of Black Males in American Society   23
Prisons Without Walls• The Black Male as Sexual Predator
• Embracing the Image • The Consequences of Adaptation

2: How Black Boys Are Raised   41
Thomas • Child-Rearing Strategies • The Warrior
Method of Raising Black Boys • The Ten Commitments
of the Warrior Method

3: Necessary Tools for African Warriors   63
NWA • The Four Cs

**4: The Seasons of Our Sons: Spring, Conception
to Four**   102
Conception Through Four Years • Black Boys at Birth •
Naming Our Children • Early Hurdles for Black Boys

5: The Seasons of Our Sons: Summer, Ages 5–12   112
Ages 5–12: Chad • Massaging the Numbers •
Violence, Health, and Athletics • Mental
Health and Black Boys • Young Warriors Councils

6: The Seasons of Our Sons: Autumn, Ages 13–21   147
The Notion of "Adolescence" • Rites of Passage •
Rob • Black Rage Revisited • Black Adolescent
Health • Autumn Warriors Councils • Educational
Issues • Work • Black Men and Women • Conclusion

**7: The Seasons of Our Sons: Winter, Ages 22
Through Homegoing**   178
Harold • We Are the Men Our Ancestors Prayed For •
Role Models • What Can Black Men and Women Learn
About Each Other? • Healthy Black Relationships:
Beloved in Our Lives

8: A Summary of the Seasons   192

9: Epilogue   200
Parable of the White Elephant

Appendix A: Annotated Bibliography   209
**Appendix B: Annotated Bibliography of Books
  for Black Children**   217
Index   221

Foreword

On a sunny, palm-covered road during the spring of 1839, Sengbeh Pieh, his wife, son, and two daughters set out from their
farm in Sierra Leone for a neighboring village. Suddenly four
black men rushed out of the trees and ambushed them. Sengbeh's wife was smashed across the face as she struggled, and the
children cried out as they watched their father dragged away.
Slavery was not unknown in this region, and Pieh, who would be
renamed "Joseph Cinque" by his captors, had been warned
about the dangers of enslavement by Europeans and the brain-
washed Africans collaborating with them in the hellish enter-
prise. Torn away from his wife and children, Sengbeh, the son of
a Mende king, was beaten into submission and taken to Lom-
boko Island, an infamous slave port a few miles off the coast of
Sierra Leone. There he was sold to a wealthy Spanish trader,
then chained below the deck of the slave ship *Iesora* to begin the
horrific Middle Passage to the Caribbean.

African cooperation with Europeans during slavery is often

discussed, but rarely understood. Slavery created an entirely
new class of Africans who sold and traded human beings as readily as they sold and traded cocoa and groundnuts. Over the
years, many whites have asked me with curiosity, "Weren't the
Africans themselves responsible for slavery, since they sold their
own people to Europeans?" I am quite sure that when whites
ask this question, they are seeking partial absolution for the sins
of their ancestors. When black people ask it, I shake my head
and wonder if they are direct descendants of Mayagilalo, the
African responsible for Cinque's capture in the first place. What
is exaggerated about African complicity in the slave "trade" is
that Africans had much choice in the matter. This is similar to
making the indigenous people who scouted for Custer responsible for the establishment of reservations in Montana years later.
These questioners would have us think that the entire population of the west coast of Africa, where most blacks in the *Maafa*[1]
originate, was involved with the slave trade. The fact is that very
few Africans were directly involved, and the tiny minority who
were could not have done it without the absolute cooperation of
Europeans. The converse is not true. Europeans had the power
to get their workers with or without the cooperation of Africans.
They needed laborers, and Africans were available. The deracinated West Africans collaborating in the slave trade at first found
cooperation with the Europeans difficult, eventually easy, and
ultimately destructive.

What is most amazing about the Middle Passage is that anyone survived at all. Eyewitness accounts of the voyage are filled

---

[1] A Kiswahili term translated as "great suffering" and increasingly used by blacks to
describe the horrors and impact of enslavement. It is preferred over "Black Holocaust"
since those wishing to confine "Holocaust" to the genocide against Jews and others during
World War II criticize the use of this term. The term denotes the *continued* suffering
endured by Africans throughout the world, is not confined to one historical event and will
be used throughout this book.

with descriptions of death, disease, rape, and torture. Rebellions by the enslaved Africans were frequent but mostly unsuccessful, and the panic that gripped the captives was nearly matched by the crews who lived in constant fear of insurrections. About three hundred people from various parts of West Africa were crowded aboard the *Iesora*. Voices of Yoruba, Ibo, Akan, Wolof, Ewe, and other Mende could be heard as the frightened and angry Africans made their way through the "doors of no return." These doors were chiseled into the slave dungeons where Africans were held before being crammed aboard the slave ships that distributed them in South America, the Caribbean, and North America. The doors were usually about five feet high and two feet across so that only one African could move through at a time, making it easier for them to be counted. Blood can still be seen on the stone walls of the dungeons. Scars crisscross the doors where the Africans clawed at the wood and resisted their captors as they were stuffed into dungeons reeking of filth and populated by vermin in the Castles of Ghana and the infamous slave port at Gorée Island off the coast of Senegal. This was their last view of Africa as they began the Middle Passage. Cinque grew up hearing tales about how the white man ate Africans, and many of the captured men and women believed that these people were from a land where food was scarce. Cinque must have thought of this, but wanted desperately to believe his elders who told him that the lands beyond the seas needed workers. He and his fellow captives must have wondered what type of work the white man was doing that he needed to travel so many moons to steal black people away from their families.

The worst part of the two-month voyage was the stench aboard the ships. A consistent thread that runs through all of the narratives written by captors and captives is the ever-present "bloody flux," a severe form of diarrhea that afflicted both slaver and slave. The Africans probably ached for the cool rivers of their villages to wash away the odor and filth that blackened their skin even further. The heat at this time was often unbearable, only worsening the smell of the waste, blood, vomit, and flux. The human cargo must have thought that God had forsaken them. Head and pubic lice added to their torment. Though the sexes were separated, the men could hear the women's cries of pain and agony as the sailors and captains casually raped and sodomized them. Many of the men and women prayed to their ancestors asking them to join them; and as the ship tossed back and forth on the waters on rainy days, Cinque's thoughts must surely have turned to his wife and children, who by now had been separated from him for two weeks. About two hundred aboard the ship survived the journey.

Three months later Joseph Cinque was sold in Havana to Jose Ruiz and Pedro Montez, wealthy Spanish plantation owners who lived in Porto Principe, a Cuban town about three hundred miles from Havana. Cinque and his comrades were purchased in early June 1839, and at eight o'clock on the evening of June 28, he and fifty-two other Africans were marched aboard the chartered schooner *Amistad*. Captain Raymond Ferrer, a small crew of two sailors, a sixteen-year old cabin boy named Antonio, and a "mulatto" cook named Celestino set sail for the four-day journey to Porto Principe. The Africans were left unchained in the hold of the ship; whether this was due to Ferrer's incompetence or ignorance, it watered the seeds of rebellion already growing among the captive Africans. Except for the uncomfortable iron collars around their necks, the Africans were free of shackles. Confidence in his small crew and the chained hatch that held the human cargo during most of the journey probably led him to believe that rebellion was only a remote possibility. I believe that

Ferrer's arrogance led him to think that by the time the Africans had gotten used to their "freedom" below deck, they would be in Porto Principe. Cinque was increasingly restless for the desired rebellion that must have been rolling around in his head for nearly three months. Certainly, the conditions on the *Amistad* were far better than on the *Iesora,* but during the months of his ordeal, he learned to be skeptical about anything the white man offered him, even if it seemed better than the previous evil. He refused to adapt to conditions that were not of his making and in later testimony would tell how much he worried about his family during his ordeal. Freedom for Cinque would always be more than simply sleeping unshackled below the deck of a ship.

Ferrer, a seasoned captain, told Ruiz and Montez that the journey would take two days. Almost immediately upon leaving Havana, the sky began to darken and the wind was replaced by a sweltering haze. Captain Ferrer decided to steer the sleek black schooner along the Cuban coast to its destination. This sailing course, he thought, would allow him to pull into shore quicker than if he were out on the high seas; British warships were known to seize Spanish vessels on a whim looking for illegal contraband and evidence of slaves. On the second day of the journey, fearing that the supplies would run out, Ferrer ordered the slaves' provisions cut, reducing the Africans' already meager rations by half. Ferrer began to worry about the restlessness of his human cargo as the wind blew against the *Amistad*'s sails, further extending their journey. Anxious as he was to rid his ship of the slaves, he was still reluctant to turn out to sea because of the British warships, so he kept the *Amistad* hugging the Cuban shore and opted for the slower journey with less wind.

On July 1, four days into his journey, Cinque's anxiety was further fueled by Celestino, who played a nasty trick on him.

Cinque asked the cook what was going to happen to them when they reached their destination. In answer, Celestino pointed to a row of beef-filled barrels, placed the knife he'd been using to chop vegetables against his throat, and pretended to slice it. Cinque's blood ran cold. This gesture confirmed his fear that white men ate Africans due to a shortage of meat in their homelands. Thoroughly taken by Celestino's cruel charade, Cinque decided that he'd rather risk his life than take the chance that Celestino was right. Walking away from the cook, Cinque spied a loose nail and hid it, hoping that he could use it as a key to the shackle around his neck. Later, working with his close friend Grabeau in the darkness below the deck, they managed to free themselves and the others. They crept stealthily into the kitchen and made weapons of the sugarcane knives that would now never be used by them in the cane fields.

At 4:00 A.M. Ferrer was jolted awake by shouts and screams on the upper deck of the ship. Jumping from his bed, he ran out of his cabin, only to be stopped by Cinque brandishing a cane knife. Ruiz and Montez, also awakened by the commotion, ran from their cabins and saw Cinque advancing on the captain. According to Ruiz's later testimony, Ferrer produced a dagger from below his tunic and, foolishly thinking that Cinque wanted more food, yelled at the slave owner to throw him some bread. Cinque looked contemptuously at the basket of bread, then ignored Ferrer's dagger, swung the sugarcane knife, and struck a ferocious blow to the captain's arm. Cinque then ordered his comrades to strangle the captain while he lay writhing on the floor. The entire battle was over in forty-five minutes. Gesturing emphatically to the captured crew, Cinque made his demands known—Ruiz and Montez were to take them back to Africa immediately.

The two took advantage of the Africans' ignorance of navigation; during the day they steered ever so slowly due east, but at night, they maneuvered the ship north by northwest. After two months of deceptive navigation toward the East Coast of the United States, Cinque's hijacked ship was forced into port off the shores of Long Island. After eight weeks on the high seas, the *Amistad*'s sails had been reduced to rags. Provisions were low, and eight Africans had died after consuming medicinal supplies in an effort to quench their thirst. Coming ashore on Long Island, Cinque and several companions agreed to surrender to authorities, thinking they would be sympathetic to what had happened to them during the past three months. These notions were soon dashed when Lieutenant Richard Meade aboard the U.S.S. *Washington* ordered the *Amistad* and its captives to be taken to Connecticut, where slavery was still allowed.

The entire affair quickly escalated into an international incident involving the United States, Spain, and Africa. Spain was outraged because their "property"—the *Amistad* and its captives—had been illegally seized by Cinque. Sierra Leonians were enraged because one of their citizens had been captured, even though the British had declared the capital Freetown—and by default the entire country—a haven for runaway Africans who had been enslaved. For the United States, the *Amistad* Africans were not only stirring the national debate on slavery, but they were also fueling tensions with England, due to the imperialist tone of the 1823 Monroe Doctrine, and with Spain, because of the defeat of the Mexicans at the Alamo just three years earlier. A grand jury was quickly convened in Hartford, Connecticut, in late September 1839, before the dispute escalated irreversibly.

The ensuing two-year legal battles brought together some of

the greatest legal minds of the day to decide the fate of the Africans who'd taken over the *Amistad*. Curious onlookers paid the equivalent of $1.90 in today's currency to view the Africans as they exercised in the yard of the New Haven prison where they were held. However, because of what they perceived as a daring and ingenious act, whites feared Cinque and held him in solitary confinement. Many comparisons were made between Cinque and Nat Turner, who only eight years previously had led on land a similar rebellion that claimed the lives of more than sixty whites. Grudging admiration from even the most hostile quarters was showered upon the "black pirate," who had almost immediately achieved mythical status throughout the United States.

There was no corridor of power untouched by the case, and Cinque and his companions were the catalysts for consolidating the fledgling abolitionist movement, which had been fractionalized by various ideologies ranging from the conservative writings of William Lloyd Garrison to the call for an outright slave rebellion by David Walker. This was America's first civil rights case, and the divided abolitionist movement united to free Cinque. They reasoned that if it could be proven that he was not "property," as the Spanish claimed, and was free to return to his homeland, the claim could then be made that all Africans in America should have the same free status. This rather naive view of the American judicial system did not, of course, take into consideration the intractability of slavery and the racism that fueled it.

Lewis Tappan, one of the leaders of the burgeoning abolitionist movement and a wealthy businessman, hired the best lawyers to defend the captives and made sure that their case remained front-page news during the first trial. President Martin Van Buren, aiming to shore up his vote with the slaveholding states where legislators were unsure about his stand on slavery, failed in his attempt to transfer custody of the *Amistad* captives to the Spanish, since the United States had no formal extradition treaty with Spain. The Monroe Doctrine of 1823 had increased tensions between Spain and the United States considerably, since it stated explicitly that Spain was to curb its expansionism in the Caribbean and South America. It contained a message of solidarity between the North and South American continents that Spain resented, and attempts to resolve international law issues such as extradition were overshadowed by the anger felt by Spain toward America's alliance with Latin America. Spain was willing to go to war over the incident and, through its ambassador, Calderon de la Barca, issued four demands to Secretary of State John Forsyth regarding Cinque and the other captured Africans:

1st. That the vessel be immediately delivered up to her owner, together with every article found on board at the time of her capture by the *Washington,* without any payment being exacted on the score of salvage, nor any charges made, than those specified in the treaty of 1795, article 1st.

2d. That it be declared that no tribunal in the United States has the right to institute proceedings against, or to impose penalties upon, the subjects of Spain, for crimes committed on board a Spanish vessel, and in the waters of the Spanish territory.

3d. That the negroes [sic] be conveyed to Havana, or be placed at the disposal of the proper authorities in that part of Her Majesty's dominions, in order to their being tried by the Spanish laws which they have violated; and that, in the mean time, they be kept in safe custody, in order to prevent their evasion.

4th. That if, in consequence of the intervention of the authorities of Connecticut, there should be any delay in the desired delivery of the vessel and the slaves, the owners both of the latter and of the former be indemnified for the injury that any accrue to them.

> —Mr. Calderon to Mr. Forsyth, 6th September, 1839, and translation. U.S. Congress. House. Africans Taken in the *Amistad*. 26th Congress, 1st session, 1840.H. Doc. 185.

Americans were split along sectional and racial lines over the decision. The *New Orleans Times-Picayune* referred to Cinque as a "black piratical murderer," while abolitionists considered him a hero. Several exchanges between Spain and the United States resulted in the United States having the last word by allowing the trial to proceed in Connecticut.

In November 1839, Americans throughout the United States listened to Cinque's testimony in rapt attention, and his words were well conveyed. His black translator, James Covey, was located by Professor Josiah Willard Gibbs of the Yale Divinity School, and spoke perfect English and Mende. A reporter for the *New Haven Daily Herald* wrote the following about Cinque as he gave his testimony:

This Cinquez [sic] is one of those spirits who appear but seldom. Possessing far more sagacity and courage than his race generally do, he had been accustomed to command. . . . His lips are thicker and more turned up than those of his race in general, but when opened display a set of teeth rivaling in beauty the most regular of those which we praise so much in Caucasian beauty. But his nostrils are the most remarkable feature he possesses. These he can contract or dilate at pleasure. His general deportment is free from levity and many white men might take a lesson in dignity and forbearance from the African Chieftain.

In January 1840, a miracle occurred: the Africans won. Judge Andrew Judson ruled in their favor and set them free. Cinque had echoed during the trial that "we are men, too!" and evidently Judson believed him when he noted that the Africans were born free and should remain such. It is clear from existing court records and newspapers that the reaction to the verdict was swift and divided on racial and sectional lines in a country wrestling with the problem of what to do with its enslaved Africans. Van Buren was incensed and, along with Spain, ordered an immediate appeal to the United States Supreme Court. Abolitionists Joshua Levitt and Lewis Tappan knew that they had to secure the services of an esteemed lawyer to argue the case; who better to do this than the venerable orator John Quincy Adams, former president of the United States. He took the appeal case reluctantly, now seventy-three years old and in ill health, and for the next year became thoroughly versed in the first civil rights case to reach the Supreme Court. His thirteen-hour long presentation to the court in February 1841 was nothing short of brilliant, since it focused on the issue of property rights rather than the thorny issue of the legality of slavery.

. . . [the Africans] were in distress, and were brought into our waters by their enemies, by those who sought, and who are still seeking, to reduce them from freedom to slavery, as a reward for having spared their lives in the fight. If the good offices of the government are to be rendered to the proprietors of shipping in distress, they are due to the Africans only, and the United States are now bound to restore the ship to the Africans and replace the Spaniards on board as prisoners.

> —Adams, John Quincy. Argument before the Supreme Court of the United States in the Case of the United States, Appellants, vs. Cinque and Other Africans Captured in the Schooner Amistad (Delivered 24 Feb. and 1 Mar. 1841). New York: W. W. Benedict, 1841.

One week later, on March 9, 1841, the justices upheld the verdict of the lower court. Several of the Africans thanked Adams for his help. Letters by two of the captives, one by Kali and one signed by Cinque, containing his only extant handwriting, are especially noteworthy:

Mr. John Q. Adams

Farmington, May, 5th, 1841

Dear Friend.

We thank you very much because you make us free because you love all Mende people. They give you money for Mende people and you say you will not take it because you love Mende people. We love you very much and we will pray for you when we rise upon the morning and when we lie down at night. We hope the Lord will love you very much and take you up to heaven when you die. We pray for all the good people who make us free. Wicked people want to make us slaves but the Great God who has made all things raise up friends for Mende people. He give us Mr. Adams that he may make us free and all Mende people free. Mr. Adams we write our names for you

Kali

Mr. Adams

We write our names for you in this Bible that you may remember Mende people. Some cannot write so we write for them.

(Signed)

Kali   Cinque   Cici   Kinna Falanna
Burmah   Fagino   Batu

Though Cinque and his brothers and sisters were finally set free, their ordeal was far from over. Van Buren, apoplectic in the White House at the verdict, refused to grant the freed Africans passageway home. The American Missionary Association (AMA), formed by Tappan and other abolitionists during the trial, became responsible for raising money to secure passage back to Sierra Leone. In its most famous work, the AMA was to establish several historically black colleges and institutions throughout the United States: most notably, Atlanta University, Fisk, Talladega, and Tougaloo. Cinque and several of the other Africans raised money for the journey home by touring the northeastern United States for nearly a year. The "lecture tour" took on a sideshow appearance in some cities, because curious onlookers simply wanted to see the Africans speaking English. In November, after earning the money for the passage home, Cinque and several other Mende set sail for Sierra Leone. They arrived there in January 1842, two and a half years after being forced into slavery. He never saw his wife or daughters again, but late in life he reunited with his son, Kolima.

Joseph Cinque's spirit lives on in his sons, America's African-American men and boys. Historians are divided as to whether or not he was aware of the events that took place in the United States after his return to Sierra Leone. We are sure that he knew about the founding of several universities because of the American Missionary Association's efforts to educate the newly freed slaves. Surely, he must have known about the end of the American Civil War that "emancipated" his brothers and sisters still chained to the land that held Africa's descendants. Perhaps he was also aware of the rise of the Ku Klux Klan, which was lynching his sons and brothers, and the Jim Crow laws that were disenfranchising them from all institutions. He would be surprised, however, to see how his children have fared since his death a little over a century ago. . . .

Prologue

I am pleased to introduce *The Warrior Method,* a very timely and pertinent book, a tool to help inspire and motivate our young African-American men to engage themselves constructively in positive choices in spite of what may seem to be insurmountable obstacles. Nothing is permanent because change is inevitable; therefore, we must not only anticipate change but also facilitate it. This is something *The Warrior Method* can do—help facilitate change in America.

The plight of our young men globally is precarious, and we must make a concentrated effort to redirect the path to adulthood that many of our sons are taking. As elders, we must become positive role models for our youth if they are to be future leaders. We must facilitate programs and teach from our own experiences to enhance their knowledge, attitude, and action toward family in particular and toward society in general. This knowledge must be packaged into "education for service" that we can then use to improve the quality of life for our society and ourselves.

Our sons' education should be shaped by an attitude that enhances their self-esteem and their self-actualization. Lessons from history, like the story of Sengbeh Pieh, who was called Joseph Cinque in America, and his colleagues, should motivate them to analyze their situation more critically and take calculated risks to improve their chances of success. Improving and expanding our knowledge of our history, understanding our contributions to America and the world, and combating the many fallacies surrounding black men in America will not only enhance our attitude but will also ensure that we are less destructive to ourselves and our community.

Knowledge, attitude, and responsible action will not only enhance the quality of life for individuals, but also invariably enhance the quality of life for all people. Miseducation and brainwashing are strategies societies use to conquer and control people and then exploit their resources for economic gain. Slavery brings with it not only physical chains but psychological chains as well. These psychological chains then form a link from one generation to the next, enslaving minds while restricting freedom. With knowledge and perseverance, people will take risks, even with fate. We must now take advantage of opportunities that will empower us to take back what is rightfully ours, take full advantage of our gifts as a people and a race, and direct our young men not only to achieve the glory of their ancestors but to surpass it. The key to the shackle around your neck is within your reach. It always has been.

It is time to take charge of our lives and to redirect the course of our sons' lives. It is never too late. My great-grandfather Sengbeh Pieh chose to change the direction of his life's journey even though the odds seemed insurmountable. With one decision, Rosa Parks changed not only the course of her life but also the course of history. If each one of us chose to change the course of just one young man's life, we would ultimately change the course of American history and our place within it.

Eliciting this change can be as simple as looking toward Africa. Many good things and people have come out of the Motherland. The Margai family led Sierra Leone to independence from the British. The Carew family led the Sierra Leone United Methodist Church Conference to independence from America. The Nkrumah family led the independence movement in Ghana and in most West African states. The Piehs are distinguished in many fields such as education, public administration, medicine, public health, customer relations, criminal justice, and religion. All of Sengbeh Pieh's descendants continue to influence lives, even in America today.

Sengbeh and his colleagues were agents of change in world history. By seizing the moment, Africans ignited the revival of the abolitionist movement, which was nearing collapse due to competing ideologies. The case of Sengbeh Pieh and his colleagues, commonly referred to as the *Amistad* case, is regarded as America's first civil rights case. This case facilitated unity among the divided abolitionist movement whose influence on education and freedom of Africans worldwide is still felt today. Educational, religious, and spiritual institutions evolved in West Africa and the southern states of America as a result of the *Amistad* case. It was because of this coalition and partnership with other people of conscience that Sengbeh and the other Africans were able to return home. It takes a village of people who want to improve quality of life for the entire community to raise productive children. The responsibility is great but not impossible because, as the *Amistad* case teaches us, anything is possible.

Though Sengbeh lost his wife and daughters, he was able to reunite with his son, Kolima. Later they would evangelize the Mende people. Sengbeh had a lot of difficulties trying to represent Europeans to his Mende countrymen. His frustration and disappointment forced him to retire into the Sherbro land in southern Sierra Leone where he is reported to have died in 1879. Kolima and his wife, Mee kema, were caught up in the Hot Tax war with the British in 1898. Several American missionaries were killed on the bank of the Taia River in Mende land. Only Peter, one of Kolima's children, attended mission schools in Taiama and Rotifunk. Peter went on to teach in the American Missionary Schools, where he served for over twenty years and later became a pastor himself. Today, Taiama has a primary school, secondary school, and the largest United Methodist church in Sierra Leone. From all indications, the efforts of the first American missionaries who returned to Sierra Leone with Sengbeh Pieh and the other Africans were the reason that the mission work in Sierra Leone became sustainable. Most of the early Europeans died, but the African-American missionaries survived and helped Sengbeh and the others venture out into Mende land. If you believe in freedom, then you must promote it; you must not rest until all enslaved people, whether physically, spiritually, or mentally enslaved, enjoy all its privileges.

Samuel Hingha Pieh
Great-grandson of Sengbeh Pieh

Introduction

> *In these bloody days and frightful nights when an*
> *urban warrior can find no face more despicable*
> *than his own, no ammunition more deadly than*
> *self-hate and no target more deserving of his true*
> *aim than his brother, we must wonder how we*
> *came so late and lonely to this place.*
>
> —MAYA ANGELOU

A National Crisis?

The cultural and social obstacles facing young African-American males today are huge and vastly different from those of just five years ago. If the current rate of homicidal violence among black males existed in white males, a national crisis would be declared, followed by a White House conference to address the problem. According to the U.S. Department of Justice Bureau of Justice Statistics, black males die at a rate fifteen times that of white males because of homicidal violence. Furthermore, the criminal prosecution—or is it persecution?—of black males continues unabated. In 1999, the Sentencing Project, which keeps track of incarceration rates by race and offense, reported that 32 percent of African-American males between the ages twenty and twenty-nine are in contact with the criminal justice system, i.e., indictment, incarceration, probation, or parole, as compared to 6 percent for white males and 8 percent for Latino males. Based on current rates of first incarceration, the U.S. Justice Department estimates that 28 percent of black males will enter state or federal prisons during their lifetime, compared to 16 percent of Latino males and 4.4 percent of white males. Sixty-seven percent of prison inmates were of color, compared to 65 percent in 1990, with African Americans making up 46 percent of state and federal prisoners.

If this trend continues, by the year 2015 *half* of all black men in America will be in contact with the criminal justice system via incarceration, probation, parole, or indictment. In Washington, D.C., the city with the highest concentration of upper-income blacks, the infant mortality rate among African-American children is only slightly lower than that of Bangladesh. Faced with statistics like these, it is no wonder many black parents consider it a great blessing if their sons live to see their eighteenth birthday.

Few parents outside of the African-American community truly grasp this reality, since violence is thought to be primarily a "black thing." When a black male commits a crime, it is expected; when a white male does so, it is explained. The Columbine massacre and other school shootings were followed by this country's talking heads groping for a reason as to why young white males from the suburbs were killing their classmates. The nation's media were riveted on the subject of young white males' "alienation" and subsequent violence toward classmates and viewed them as "unusual," while essentially ignoring violence among young black males. (I will later offer reasons why much of this violence is directed toward other black males.) Some sociologists now say suburbs may actually contribute to feelings of alienation for some of the children who live there. Michael Southworth, an urban design professor at the University of California at Berkeley, believes the problem of isolation is made worse by the layout of suburbs into cul-de-sacs. "You can see each of these housing tracts is really an island unto itself, with very little connectedness between them," he said. Southworth goes on to say that inner-city children have a greater sense of community and thus feel less alienated from neighbors! Insofar as murder rates are concerned, there is a remarkable decrease since 1995 of black males victimizing one another. While murder rates for all races decreased dramatically during the 1990s, according to the FBI Uniform Crime Statistics, black males as murder victims decreased by 50 percent between 1978 (when it peaked to one in forty-eight black males dying from homicide) and 1997 (when it had declined to one in sixty-eight) for men in their twenties.

The citation of these gloomy statistics is all too common when discussing black men, and I cite them here in order to redirect attention to how black males' self-destructive behavior can be attributed to the negative and stereotypical images bombarding them. Few people wish to make the connection between such self-destructive behavior and the images projected by media and other sources, yet it is even more destructive for black men to ignore these connections.

A few weeks ago, I stopped at an intersection near Fisk University and pulled up next to a young black man driving a late-model car. He gripped the steering wheel tightly, while simultaneously bouncing back and forth to the beat of the rap playing on his radio. I looked at him and smiled, and he returned the look with a scowl, yelling: "Mothafucka, what you lookin' at? I'll kill you!" He then gunned his car and took off. As I slowly drove off, I thought about what has happened to young brothers such as him, who think smiling is "soft," respect for elders is outdated, and eye contact means aggression. That thought was still with me when I got to my office. Instead of beginning my work,

I sketched out some of the self-destructive and negative black male behavior I have seen.

Destructive Black Male Behavior

The Super Slaves

Black males who occupy high positions of authority yet are so infected by white supremacy that they work against freeing others from racial oppression. They are defined by whites as being "acceptable"; in the not-to-distant past they may have been seen as a "credit to their race." They define success as the degree to which they are disconnected rather than attached to African-American culture, and find reinforcement for this in a nation that insists on blacks deracinating themselves in order to be "acceptable as Americans."

Hip–Hop Hustlers

Black males who rationalize violence and self-destructive behavior under the guise of "keeping it real." They see no connection between living the "thug life" and their obligations to black communities.

The Wanna–nevah–bees

Nearly deracinated, these persons have been variously referred to as the "black Anglo-Saxons" (Nathan Hare), "our kind of people" (Lawrence Otis Graham) and the "black bourgeoisie" (E. Franklin Frazier). It is not an automatic state of mind when achieving the sacred middle class, but it can be the inevitable result of moving away from black communities psychologically, often physically, and resulting in cultural confusion about one's identity.

The Killers

The ultimate in self-destruction among black males, the males actually wreak direct destruction on black communities in the form of selling drugs, pimping, or committing murder. They exhibit a near total absence of protective behavior toward black communities and instead view them and their residents only in terms of exploitation.

What is important to note is that the self-destructive types listed above have always existed in the African-American community. Even the Hip-Hop Hustler finds his ancestral linkages with the likes of minstrels who, though they have been romanticized as entertainers seeking to survive during the post-Reconstruction era, in many cases they actively sought compensation and ignored the critics of the music they produced. Minstrels were merely black actors portraying the images that whites had assigned them, and many rap videos do the same with the images they show of young black men. There have also been black men who could easily be graduates of Poro Societies like Cinque, men who are representative of the best in black America and are not the exception.

Constructive Black Male Behavior

The Warriors

These black men directly engage white supremacist systems. They are the civil rights leaders, community organizers, writers, and artists who leave no doubt that their protest, writings, art, and action are antiracist. Viewed by some whites and blacks as troublemakers, they see justice as a core value in their lives and speak out against various forms of racial injustice.

The Strategists

Viewed by some as "accommodationists," they are clear in their commitment to black people. They often hold positions of power and may be reluctant to take risks that involve the loss of power, but they will never work against their communities. They are the opposite of Super Slaves, who have no commitment to black people and, if given the opportunity, will actively work against their interests.

The Griots

The Malian class of storytellers, popularized by Alex Haley's *Roots,* is often viewed as a wise man preserving the history of his people through the oral tradition. Part of this is true; what frequently is neglected is that griots often lived outside the village and recorded not only the heroic stories of their clan, but its failures as well. Griots among African-American men are those who tell us who we are and who we aren't, what we should be and what we haven't been. They are the elders who have an ancestral memory of the good, bad, and ugly about black people and tell the truth no matter what the cost. They tell the truth in love, not to hurt but to heal.

The Healers

Teachers, physicians, and ministers who equip black people with knowledge of self are healers. They focus on individuals rather than systems, but have a deep understanding of how systems work, particularly as they impact black people. They are black men who never pass an opportunity to provide encouraging words to victims of racism and give psychological direction to those confused by what is happening to them.

As an educator who specializes in the development of African-American adolescents, I am constantly asked if there are any successful techniques to be used to help raise healthy, confident African-American males. Of course. But it is far from easy because psychologists and educators are reluctant to offer techniques that factor in the role of racism in the development of African-American boys. The preferred method of explaining black male behavior is to focus on internal rather than external issues that determine their lifestyles. Social scientists who point the finger at racism as a primary factor in shaping the development of black boys are perceived as being "too liberal" and as avoiding the "hard questions" that focus on biological and intellectual inequalities in African-American males. Furthermore, new research initiatives on understanding black boys continue to blame the victims. Several recent studies reflect the frustration of a society that feels this group of children has something so "wrong" with them that it offers biased research to "answer" some of the questions regarding them.

Violent behavior among black males has led certain scientists to theorize that there is a "genetic" predisposition for violence within them. In 1993, Dr. Frederick Goodwin, former director of the National Institute of Mental Health, was quoted as suggesting that inner-city "ghetto" males were like "jungle monkeys" with regard to violent behavior. Shortly after these statements, the National Institutes of Health announced plans for a conference with the proposed title "Genetic Factors in Crime: Findings, Uses and Implications" that caused a storm of protest from African Americans, including the Congressional Black Caucus, which ultimately led to its cancellation. In a similar vein, Charles Murray and Richard Herrnstein's *The Bell Curve: Intelligence and Class Structure in American Life* offers a "social science" approach to intelligence and race that theorizes how social policy should be altered to allow for the intellectual "inferiority" of blacks and Latinos. It is clear that such biased research reflects a society seeking simple answers to very complex questions. It is also clear that African Americans are often used as scapegoats when public policy has failed to provide answers to some of these problems.

Not so clear, however, is why explanations of white adolescent behavior are commonly offered in the context of how social forces shape their behavior. Mary Pipher's best-selling book *Reviving Ophelia* discusses how sexism plays a nefarious role in the development of white females, particularly as it relates to their dependence on male approval. It is nearly unthinkable to exclude social factors in explaining white adolescent behavior, yet explanations of black adolescent behavior often focus on the internal pathologies of black life in America. What is emerging is a picture of black adolescent boys that ignores how racism influences their lives. It is not black boys who must be examined, but child-rearing techniques that must be restructured so that these young males grow up healthy despite the racism that assaults them on a daily basis. What we have here is the classic question of what came first: the racist society or the dysfunctional black male?

The Poro and Sande Societies

Sengbeh Pieh and his childhood friends were fortunate to have been raised in the West African way of child rearing. The Mende created two secret societies that initiated their children into adulthood: Poro for boys and Sande for girls. When girls and boys reached their teens, they went through special training to join these organizations, learning everything that would move them into adulthood. Admission to both societies varied, with some emphasizing the ability to pay, and others opting for strong recommendations from older members' observation of certain children. Though these societies were not open to all Mende, if asked, children were encouraged to participate in this coveted rite of passage. Being a member of these societies guaranteed that the initiate would play an important role with the everyday governing of the Mende community. At age thirteen Mende boys wishing to become men paid a fee to join the Poro Society. The Sande Society taught Mende girls their responsibilities as wives, mothers, and members of the community. Older women taught the girls dancing and singing, domestic skills, child care, grooming, and etiquette, in addition to religious studies. The girls were initiated at menarche; as they grew older, they rose in rank within the society until they became a part of its administration. Adell Patton notes in his book *Physicians, Colonial Racism, and Diaspora in West Africa* that Sande-initiated women in Sierra Leone refused to allow African doctors to examine them unless they were Poro initiates.

During the Poro initiation, the boys were removed from their families for six months, from November to May, and taken by older men in the village to a remote area where they learned to hunt, farm, cook, and protect their villages. The elders believed that the boys should struggle to find answers about law, nature, religion, and life itself, with adults guiding them only when necessary. Only in the past forty years have Western psychologists proven that "active learning" is more instructive than passive learning, which is directed by the instructor—something the Mende learned a long time ago. The Poro Society taught not only mental acuity but physical endurance as well. Its members learned not only how to solve their own problems, but also how to endure pain by sleeping at night with sticks that had been soaked in water and placed under their bedclothes. They often remained outdoors when it rained. Though harsh, their ritual prepared the boys for survival under many circumstances. It conditioned them to use whatever was at hand for food, tools, and survival; and it taught them to see themselves as part of the environment rather than as a participant in it.

Poro Society also taught the young men to respect women, since life flowed from the female. Poro teachings instilled a sense of trust and mutual respect between African men and women and ensured that women were free from male violence and protected by all the men of their clan. The boys also learned the importance of working closely with girls and women and of the female's importance to the Mende culture. Both men and women cooked the meals and helped to build the homes. Though the boys' mentors explained to them the roles of husband, father, farmer, and hunter, the distinctions between male and female roles in most West African societies were blurred and in many cases nonexistent. In Poro and Sande Societies, the initiates were taught all the laws of the Mende, such as their responsibilities to their elders regardless of their medical condition. Poro also demanded that every law enacted by elders in the Poro Society should be carefully considered and not just enacted because of self-interest or monetary gain. The societies also taught the laws and customs of other tribes and cultures, and the best way to navigate these laws in trade and other legal matters. To this end, mock trials were held in front of large audiences in order to increase the young boys' confidence in public speaking—something that served Sengbeh well when he became the central figure in America's first civil rights case.

Poro Society is hundreds of years old and still exists throughout West Africa. In large parts of Guinea, Sierra Leone, and Liberia, all boys are expected to join the Poro of their local town or village when they turn thirteen. In *The Warrior Method,* I adapt parts of the Poro teachings as well as strategies specific for raising healthy black boys in our racist society. I make no apologies for including racism as a leading cause of problems encountered by them. But neither do I see racism as the only factor in shaping their development. In truth, omitting it as a causal factor in their social growth is disingenuous and perpetuates the notion of black inferiority. Raising black boys in a racist society should be viewed as a challenge to the parent and educator who truly wishes to see healthy black men develop in America as well as in other Western nations.

A few years ago, after giving a lecture at the University of London, I was struck, but not surprised, as English educators and parents shared similar experiences about their black boys in terms of learning styles, violence, and rates of truancy. It is difficult for many people to accept that the treatment of black boys in predominantly white societies around the world is remarkably consistent. They experience high rates of expulsion from schools and police brutality, and they are viewed as being dangerous. While it is easy to cite the pressures facing black boys, such as drugs, homicidal violence, and family breakdown, it is far less popular to discuss the roots of these challenges that emerge from other conditions sanctioned by racist societies.

My Own Story

Finally, the story of Cinque's sons is my story as well.

Evicted from four apartments in the years between 1950 and 1959, our family could have easily been the poster children for black poverty. In the late 1940s, my father was fired from his job at a Pittsburgh steel mill for organizing black steelworkers to resist taking the most dangerous jobs at the plants and advocating the revolutionary idea of "equal pay for equal work." In 1948, he moved the family to Cleveland to start a new life after being "whiteballed" throughout the steel industry in Pittsburgh. He joined that special group known as "bad nigger" men who were forced to leave small towns and cities quickly and often. Whenever they spoke truth to white power, they immediately lost their jobs and had to move on to find new employment, all at the whim of white supremacy.

Adding my youngest brother, Ron, to the Winbush brood broke him financially and resulted first in evictions and then in six heart attacks, the first in 1959. His anger and frustration at not being able to provide for his family were often taken out on our mother. My parents were constantly at odds over exactly what was causing their fighting and poverty. They simply didn't understand that their problems were inflamed by the racism around them. Low wages, a depressed economy, and discrimination were what contributed to the frustration between them. They were able to see this when Malcolm X and Martin Luther King, Jr. came on the scene and showed them—and the rest of black America—the enormous influence racism played in their lives.

Growing up on the east side of Cleveland during the 1960s, my brothers and I saw violence every day. We all coped with it in

different ways. These different approaches created both harmony and friction between us as we tried to share elements of
our vastly different worlds. I, the middle brother, had been fortunate enough to score high on what I later would know was the
Stanford-Binet Intelligence Test. That score enabled me to be
bused out of my poor neighborhood to an accelerated school in
a middle-class white neighborhood. I often felt like the brother
on the outside because of my privileged education at a well-
kept, predominantly white school, far from the "horrors" of
Hough Avenue. Ron, one year younger than me, was constantly
fighting off neighborhood bullies throughout both junior high
and high school. It troubled me that I went to school in a relatively safe environment while he had to fight nearly every day
just for the right to learn. He paid the price by making only fair
grades during his middle school years, but he excelled academically in high school after our parents moved us to Warrensville
Heights, a suburb that was safe, clean, and predominantly populated by working-class whites.

Academically, Ron was in a much better place, but now the
violence came from his white classmates who resented the fact
that their neighborhood was becoming a "promised land for
blacks." Forced into a fight by the leader of a group of Italian
boys who cornered him after school, Ron broke the jaw of one of
the kids, which almost resulted in *his* suspension from school.
Although fighting almost every day, Ron somehow managed to
finish high school with good grades. He went on to Cleveland
State University, where he played varsity basketball. Maintaining
his politics, Ron was arrested in 1970, as one of the "CSU Six,"
for demonstrating against neo-Nazis in support of the killings
that took place at Jackson and Kent State Universities. He then
graduated from college and went on to earn a master's degree in
social work from Case Western Reserve University. He married

a high school classmate and now lives firmly entrenched in the upper middle class of fashionable Shaker Heights, Ohio.

My brother Ron is living proof that one can be true to his politics and his people without sacrificing himself. The way Ron and I differed was that he threw the violence back into the face of whoever was dispensing it, while I tried to navigate around it by seeing it as symptomatic of what was happening to black people in general. I would later discover that both our strategies were invaluable for surviving as black boys growing up in America.

Our oldest brother, Harold, or "Windy" as we used to call him, was older than me by eleven years, and by turns both brilliant and contentious. Bored by the laissez-faire educational curriculum and apathetic teachers of Cleveland, he stopped going and instead turned to various forms of hustling and theft. His brief marriage at twenty-one resulted in divorce and a daughter. His many brushes with the law caused our parents endless grief. Some of my earliest memories of Windy consist of our visits to see him at the Work House, a Dickensian slave camp where the crime of nonpayment of child support was punished by incarceration and fifteen cents an hour in wages until it was paid off. He left the Work House only to graduate to the state penitentiary, where he did five years for first-degree manslaughter. Windy had secured a job with the state branch of the mental hospital as an orderly. He viewed it as something that would enable him to rebuild his reputation, which had been increasingly marred by petty brushes with the law. As an orderly, he did mundane chores such as shaving, dressing, and taking care of mentally ill and disturbed patients who had varying grasps on reality. Though the work was menial, Windy was proud of having and keeping a job, and he always set out for work with a spring in his step.

One night, approximately three months into his job, one of Windy's charges started taunting him, calling him "nigger" and spewing racial epithets as Windy shaved him. My brother lost control, and the years of rage that he'd kept so tightly reined in slipped. I make no excuses for Windy. I simply know that he had seen violence firsthand, and when he reached his breaking point, he couldn't hold himself back. He let the ten years of frustration, disappointment, anger, yearning, and his feelings of lack of fulfillment take control of his reason. Windy did what many black men—who have simply been pushed too far—think about doing, but thankfully rarely do. For his crime, he spent five years in prison for first-degree manslaughter.

For weeks after Windy was arrested, there was an outcry against Ohio State mental facilities. The newspapers trumpeted the story of how the institution had entrusted the lives of patients to an "ex-con." Ron and I endured the taunts from neighbors and classmates, and the drama created in me a distrust of "friends," who saw the manslaughter charges as a vehicle to tease, mock, and humiliate me as the brother of a murderer. I was involved in many fights during this time, and although I never backed down, I knew I was caught up in a strange self-fulfilling prophecy because I was reinforcing the misconception that the Winbush brothers were simply violent black men.

I corresponded with Windy while I attended Oakwood College. I always looked up to him—even when he was in prison—because he was well read, had a sharp mind, and often told me things that later came true. He warned me to be careful with the white boys I would later meet at school because they would try to make me feel inferior. He told me to read something every night about black people so that it would balance the "poison" I would read every day about white people. He also told me that debating taught one how others think: that I should debate with people I didn't trust because it would teach me more about them, and that I should avoid debating with people I did trust because it might distance me from them. He saw argument as a way of gaining knowledge and primarily reserved for persons whom you either did not know or did not trust. His knowledge and insight served me a world of good as I made my way first through Oakwood, then Harvard and Yale on summer scholarships, and finally through the University of Chicago, where I got my master's and Ph.D. in psychology, and where only eight blacks walked across the stage during my 1976 graduation ceremony.

In 1994, I had an eerie feeling of déjà vu while watching the film *The Shawshank Redemption.* Staying for the credits, I understood the feeling of recognition. The film had been shot in Mansfield Reformatory, the now abandoned penitentiary in Ohio where I often visited my brother as he served his time. As the lights went up in the theater, I considered how ability and luck had played a major role in the lives of the Winbush brothers. Ron and I were lucky that civil rights legislation dismantled walls that had prevented Windy from even dreaming about college. He had gone to school just before Rosa Parks took her sheroic sit-down against racism on a Montgomery, Alabama, bus, and just before Ron and I got the largesse of a nation attempting to atone for the sins of its past. Our scholarships to Harvard, Yale, Cleveland State, Case Western Reserve, and the University of Chicago did not exist just ten years prior to when we attended school there, and Windy might not have gone to prison had he had the same educational opportunities afforded to Ron and me. What we had in formal education, Windy compensated for by being a voracious reader. He told me in a letter never to throw away a book because I could learn something from all of them, and that I may need that knowledge in the future. I retain this obsessive habit to this day. In a letter from prison to my sister Myrna, dated March 27, 1966, Windy wrote:

One of the worst things that can happen to any individual
is when a person's freedom is denied him, or taken away. I
never realized the joy and pleasure of freedom until I
came here . . . it's a hurting feeling to be stripped of my
manhood and lose your identity as a human being . . .
there are many in here who have peace with the world.
Why? Because this is the only life they have known.
These—vegetables, that's what they are to me—have no
ambitions, no goals in life . . . I pity all of them. . . ."

Even in the bowels of "Shawshank," Windy saw himself as better
than other inmates, because prison for him was simply *where* he
was and not *who* he was.

Black boys in the 1960s were members of the last generation
of young men who had their eyes on the prize. As a group we
knew where we were supposed to go, and how to get there. Like
Windy, many of us may not have chosen the right path, or may
have let circumstances get the better of us, but we knew that
ours was the generation that was to fulfill the dreams of Du Bois,
Crummell, and Garvey. They were our heroes. We mourned the
death of JFK the way my father mourned the death of Roosevelt,
but we did not name our sons "Kennedy" the way my father's
generation had named their sons "Roosevelt," in tribute to their
fallen hero. We changed our names to "Muhammad," "Kahlil,"
and "Amiri," and traded in our "slave names" for an "X."

Our eyes were turning east to Africa in ways that had not
been seen since Marcus Garvey's Back to Africa movement in
the 1920s. Black men were wearing dashikis, although no such
clothes existed in Africa. We celebrated the naturalness of our
kinky, nappy, and locked hair, and, finally, black became beautiful. West Africa was the place to vacation as much as Grandma's

southern home during the summer. Cassius Clay became Muhammad Ali, and Stokely Carmichael took the name Kwame Toure, moved to Guinea Bissau, and reinforced the idea that living in Africa was a viable alternative to living with the racism in America. In 1961, Du Bois moved to Ghana, and Nkrumah encouraged others to do the same. Black boys heard their fathers openly revere and criticize Dr. King, for they were both awed and appalled by his militant nonviolence.

The story of *The Warrior Method* is the story of all black men in America, and their sons as well. My story, the story of three black boys growing up in Cleveland, Ohio, during the 1950s and 1960s, is one of opportunity, chance, and blind fate; it mirrors the experiences of all black boys in America. Though far more intelligent than I, Windy ended up in prison while I ended up at Harvard. Our fates were nothing more nor less than circumstances and opportunities. The opportunities given to me were a gift and a godsend, and they enabled me to live up to my potential. But I was one out of hundreds. I wonder what Windy would have done with them, who he would have become, what would have been his contributions? Opportunities like these—education, safe schools, a congenial learning environment—are the norm for white boys who are given the chance to succeed daily; while black boys have to fight daily, just for the right to learn or the chance to dream.

I wonder what America would be like today if all of Cinque's sons were given the opportunity and the resources for achievement? And I wonder what America will be like for my sons, Omari and Faraji. . . .

1

The Image of Black Males in American Society

Being a black man in America is like being a spectator at your own lynching.   —ISHMAEL REED

Prisons Without Walls

I had just finished a daylong speaking engagement at a prison in a very rural area of south-central Tennessee. It was almost dusk as I made my final comments to a group of incarcerated black men. I listened to their stories about how they'd found themselves in this lonely rural place where the "strange fruit" of their ancestors had hung on trees in the not-too-distant past. As I said my good-byes, I was pleased that we'd all come to realize how much we had in common as black men. In addition, I was thrilled that they had entrusted me with information, greetings, and letters to send to their families, parole boards, and friends in the "free world." I, in turn, took their addresses and promised to keep in touch. I then said my farewells and started on my journey home, up the very dark and meandering road away from the prison.

I got lost almost immediately. The inky blackness of the

Tennessee woods, complete with kudzu-laden trees, gave eerie shapes to the thick undergrowth hovering over the two-lane highway in the middle of nowhere. I made a decision to stop at the first light I encountered, which came after driving nearly five miles. I pulled into a country gas station and noted how fast the bugs were flying around the lights illuminating the convenience store. As I got out of my car, I suddenly felt more connected to my brothers whom I had just left. Inside the store I saw a white man with a red baseball hat, peering curiously through the window at me. I looked beyond him farther into the store and saw two white women sitting behind a counter. In that split second, it occurred to me that one of them was clutching an object beneath the well-worn table. I realized that the object was a gun and that I was dangerous in their eyes simply because I was a black man entering their store at night. To them I was out of context. It happens to black men when we drive into an all-white neighborhood, walk into a restaurant in an area where serving black men is both rare and unexpected, or simply when we try to get directions when lost.

I quickly "assumed the position," placing my hands where they could easily be seen on the glass door, and walked in. As I entered the store and casually asked the man for directions, I could feel the tension. His Tennessee drawl sketched a vague picture of where the interstate might be. While I listened, I suddenly realized that the only reason I had entered the store, after seeing their looks of fear, was to dispel the notion that I was intent on either robbing or killing them.

I thanked him for the directions, and then, without thinking, turned and asked the woman what she was holding behind the counter. I was surprised at my own words even as they left my mouth, knowing that my question could easily be interpreted as a way of sizing them up before I committed my crime. "A gun," she replied quite calmly. Stepping deeper into the racial abyss, I asked her if she thought I was going to rob her. In the same Tennessee monotone she answered, "Yes."

Her two companions moved closer to her behind the counter, and I recklessly continued. More from a race-fatigued haze than from bravado, I asked if she'd assumed, because I was black, that I was going to rob her. She paused a moment and, in a low voice, said, "To be honest, yes." They all looked at me, and for a split second, I could see plainly their embarrassment, anger, and bewilderment. I felt strangely empowered. Just a few moments earlier, I'd felt powerless and somehow at fault simply for being a black man. But as we all stood there looking at one another and barely breathing, I felt in control. I had reacted honestly when confronted by their discrimination and stereotypical images of black men. I took a breath and then asked if they could spare a few minutes to talk to me about what just happened, and what could have happened but thankfully hadn't. Surprisingly, they said they could.

Though I do not remember exactly the words exchanged during the next twenty minutes or so, what I do remember quite clearly is that all three talked extensively about how their impressions of black males had been formed by a witches' brew of stereotypes, television, folklore, hatred, and misunderstandings. They all had the same fears—due mostly to ignorance—of black-on-white crime and interracial sexual couplings. After we'd talked for a few minutes, they began to ask me questions that no one in their white world could answer with any degree of certainty or authenticity. They were curious to know my feelings about O. J., Tupac, Colin, Louis, Michael, and many other black males. As we talked, they expressed deep-seated beliefs passed on from their parents and peers, fallacies such as the black man's sexual and athletic prowess, his wanton and overriding lust for white women, and the black woman's sexual promiscuity. Neighborhoods will deteriorate and schools will decline if blacks were allowed to "move in," they told me. It seemed as if all of the misinformation they had heard and repeated to one another was now ready to be shared with the one black man who happened to wander into their store that night.

I listened closely to all that they said, and I realized that only a moment before these same people had been prepared to shoot me, and probably would not have gone to jail if they had. Their ignorance had made them just as afraid of black people in general, and black men in particular, as their predecessors had been when D. W. Griffith shot *The Birth of a Nation,* when the Scottsboro Boys were tried, when Emmett Till was lynched, or when Willie Horton became the poster child for black men. These people were afraid of me for no reason at all. And had it not been for my pausing to discuss their fears, they simply would have wondered what a black man was doing in "their" town so late at night, out of the context in which they had cast him.

After about twenty or thirty minutes, the man said, apologetically, that it was time to close the store. I embraced the idea quicker than the woman did, and said that I needed to be on my way before it got any darker. We lied to one another about stopping by if either was in the other's area. Then I walked into the cool night, glad that one more time I had escaped death from the hands of the white men who had stereotyped notions of black men. I know many black men who have had similar escapes, and I know of too many others who didn't.

The American propaganda machine has been thorough, on so many levels, in poisoning the minds of insecure whites about black males. The results of this stereotyping have yielded a complex web of images for black boys. In a recent poll by the National Opinion Research Center, 56 percent of Americans reported that they thought blacks were "more dangerous" than whites. Much of this perceived "dangerousness" on the part of whites can be understood by anatomizing the nexus between race and sex in American history.

The Black Male as Sexual Predator

"Lazy," "shiftless," "violent," "gangsta," "hoodlum," "stud," "invisible," "stupid," "entertaining," "superathlete," "dangerous." If this were the extent of the list of adjectives and nouns used to describe contemporary African-American males, perhaps young blacks could resist the powerful message it sends to them. Unfortunately, the list goes on and on. Black males grow up with the knowledge that society in general believes them to be mostly worthless if they are not superathletes or entertainers, and that they are limited in what they can achieve.

Every day nearly all forms of media assault African-American boys with the notion that they are simply no good. Black men handcuffed on the eleven o'clock news, "gangsta" rappers with platinum fangs in their mouths, exaggerated images of young black males being arrested for drugs provide daily doses of negative images to young black boys. Images that serve to reinforce negative stereotypes that black males are insane take the form of a racially/sexually confused Dennis Rodman, a misguided Michael Jackson, and an army of rap artists who stare into the camera during their videos with threatening postures while they call black women "bitches" and their brothers "dawgs" and "niggahs." The "thinking black male" is seen at best as quirky or at worst as an aberration. This "Urkelization" of intelligent black men is seen in Ving Rhames's portrayal of an electronic genius in the film *Mission: Impossible*. His character seldom speaks, is sexless, and has encyclopedic knowledge on the most esoteric of things. Although viewed as a "strong black man," he was gang-raped and sodomized by white men in the cult classic *Pulp Fiction*, became a caricature of Johnnie Cochran in *American Tragedy*, the only TV miniseries dramatizing the O. J. Simpson case, and was reduced to tears at the 1998 Golden Globe Awards, even giving his gleaming statuette to someone "more deserving," in the form of fellow actor Jack Lemmon. Hollyweird, as Chuck D of Public Enemy calls it, has a way of whittling down even the strongest images of black men to blubbering and sexless creatures.

The elevation of George Washington Carver to mythic status by white teachers, while emphasizing pride in the genius of the "Wizard of Tuskegee," inadvertently portrays him as an *exceptional* genius with scientific feats that could hardly be duplicated by the average black man. Intellectual achievements of black men are not ignored; they are *exceptionalized* into the realm of the extraordinary. Even a young Tiger Woods, who fantasized about his "Cablanasian" ancestry in a sport that paid homage to intelligence, is not immune from sports commentators noting his "tremendous strength" in driving the ball, as opposed to the traditional references of "keen intellect" that are reserved for white golfers. Michael Jordan was more endowed with wondrous physical agility than intellect. Wynton Marsalis's facility with both jazz and European classical music is seen as a "gift," even though Marsalis argues that a riff in jazz is far more difficult to play than a Bach fugue.

This disparagement of the black male intellect and the emphasis on his physical attributes has a long history. Their physicality is believed to be the only part of black men worth discussing. This constant and universal narrative began with the initial encounters that European explorers had with Africa.

Winthrop Jordan, in his classic work *White Over Black,* presents numerous documents written during the European colonization of Africa where explorers wrote back to their home country about the extraordinarily "long tailes" of "wild" black men in the "jungles of black Africa."

Welsing argues, as does Dutch scholar Jan Nederveen Pieterse in his book *White on Black,* that the sexual image of black men was unconsciously *and* consciously shaped by white men in literature, anthropology, and history to distort and particularly to exaggerate their prowess in order to create in white females the fear of rape by black men. He argues that "protecting white women"—a persistent theme in the history of European racism—is a reflection of the insecurity that white males have of the black penis.

This "black man will rape you" anxiety, a persistent American theme, was placed squarely at the forefront of American politics during the 1988 presidential elections. The late Lee Atwater, campaign manager for George Bush, used it in the infamous Willie Horton political ads to swing the white "female vote," which had been leaning heavily toward Michael Dukakis. Horton, convicted of raping and killing a white woman during a weekend pass from prison, was employed in political ads that effectively siphoned white female votes away from Dukakis. In an interview with *Life* magazine just before his death, Atwater admitted that the ploy in the commercials was to present Dukakis as "being soft" on black criminals. Going for the racial jugular vein by presenting Mr. Horton as the embodiment of the Great White Fear—black men raping and killing white women—worked, swinging a significant portion of the female vote to George Bush. The rest is history.

Susan Gubar says that white parodies of black life are so endemic to America that they are unconsciously reflected in art, literature, and film. She cites the example of a colleague teaching at an Ivy League university who confided in her that her husband spoke "black talk" to their dog. She says that sexuality in particular creates anxiety among white Americans so much so that its expression is often difficult to discern. The denial of "black envy," as she calls it, borders on the pathological. She analyzes Robert Mapplethorpe's controversial 1980 photo *Man in Polyester Suit*, in which a black man clothed in a drab gray suit has his large penis hanging noticeably from his pants. Gubar argues that the black male is viewed with sexual envy throughout Western literature and that deconstructing this envy is often difficult since it challenges dearly held assumptions about black/white relationships both sexual and nonsexual. The O.J. Simpson murder trial provided yet another case of the unconscious obsession that white America has with the sexual dynamics of black men and white women. The so-called "race card" may be better identified as the "race/sex card" since these two powerful factors converged during America's most recent obsession with race and sex. The trial reinforced the notion that black male/white female sexuality is taboo because it is ultimately dangerous and often leads to death. In fact, only 3 to 4 percent of all rape is interracial (white men raping black women and black men raping white women) yet these are the cases that garner the most headlines.

Historically, the mere rumor of an interracial rape involving a black male and a white female could set the stage for a lynching. The fear of black men and white women coupling is a great determiner of social mores and shaped the image of black males in America. So pervasive is this fear among many white Americans that it is actually responsible for the founding of a "church" as well as school policy. Matthew Hale, a self-proclaimed "minister" in the World Church of the Creator, said that his motivation to establish this white supremacist church was triggered when he witnessed a white woman kissing a black man in a film. Hale was blamed for inciting Benjamin Nathaniel Smith to launch a hate-crime spree in July 1999 in Illinois and Indiana, during which two people were killed and nine wounded. Bob Jones University's policy against interracial dating is still another indicator of white anxiety over black male/white female coupling. Despite the loss of federal funds because of this policy, administrators at the university continue the long history of racism based on twisted interpretations of the Bible relative to "race mixing."

We should not, however, think that the "black male as rapist of white woman" fear is reserved only for white supremacists. Hollywood has consistently reinforced the notion of the black male as predator. D.W. Griffith's 1915 classic *The Birth of a Nation* was initially entitled *The Clansman*; the title was changed in part because he felt its appeal to Americans was far greater than the small sector of citizens found below the Mason-Dixon line. The appeal, of course, was to the primal fear in the American white psyche, that black men will rape "our" fair daughters, wives, aunts, grandmothers, and sisters if they are not held in check. Woodrow Wilson, the Ku Klux Klan's favorite president, wrote in his *History of the American People* that the film showed "the policy of congressional leaders was determined to overthrow civilization in the South, to put the white South under the heel of the black South. For self-preservation, the whites formed a group called the Ku Klux Klan, a veritable empire of the South, to protect the Southern country."

The original *King Kong*, released in 1933, illustrates the symbolic anxiety over black male and white female sexuality. Released during the height of the "Scottsboro Boys" case, in which nine black boys and men ranging in ages from thirteen to twenty-one were accused of raping two white women, the film portrays a giant crazed ape lusting after a fair white woman in distress. Kong, who had resided peacefully in the African rain forest for an unknown period, suddenly goes wild (ape?) over a white female accompanying an expedition to his prehistoric island. Several authors have pointed out the nature of the phallus represented by the ape's ascension to the top of the then newly erected Empire State Building, and the subsequent killing of the monster by pilots is a symbolic castration and lynching of black men, still prevalent in America at the time of the film. Far-fetched though it may seem, it provides an intriguing analysis of Hollywood's endorsement of the idea of black men as sexual predators. Lending credibility to this assertion is the fact that it was released in Nazi Germany during this same period as *King Kong und die Weisse Frau* (*King Kong and the White Woman*).

Although they exist, persons creating media images usually deny sexual/racial symbolism, even when symbolic references are far too blatant to overlook or ignore. In *Episode I: The Phantom Menace,* the 1999 prequel to *Star Wars,* George Lucas's computer-generated creature Jar Jar Binks was heatedly denounced by several ethnic groups as a racist stereotype of black men. Similar stereotypical images exist with mock portrayals of Asian and Arabs in the film, also conveniently disguised as extraterrestrials. The producers of the film vehemently denied that the computer-generated images were racist and dismissed the charge of racism by insisting that Lucas was merely trying to portray characters that would appeal to young people. If their assertions are sincere, then it is quite telling just how deeply these images of race are embedded in our minds. Ironically, one of the most sinister characters in the film, Darth Maul, who dresses in black and is clearly a metaphor for the sinister black male, has a website on the Internet hosted mostly by white females and curiously titled the Darth Maul Estrogen Brigade (!).

The portrayal of the black male as sexual predator has served well in convincing a sexually insecure white America that, if left unchecked, black boys will "marry our daughters." The horror! This unspoken social policy of racial exclusion based on gender and race placed black males in such a precarious position that we had to monitor even our most straightforward and innocent interactions with white women. The single most commonly given "reason" for the mass lynching of black men in America was the *idea* that they had violated white women by sexual molestation. Rumors alone were enough to ignite angry white men to *defend* white womanhood by lynching, burning, and castrating *any* black male perceived as having violated this code. The burning of the black section of Tulsa, Oklahoma, in 1921 and of Rosewood, Florida, in 1923, and the lynching of Emmett Till in 1955 are three of the hundreds of racial violence incidents that had their roots in the perception of black men as "violating the sanctity" of white womanhood.

The unconscious social fear of black men's libidinous urges toward white women is a globally held perception. From Shakespeare's *Othello* to the European exploitation of Africa, this theme is played out and is important in how racial policies are established. In hearings at the Truth and Reconciliation Commission, established by Archbishop Emeritus Desmond Tutu during Nelson Mandela's presidency, it was revealed that the primary obsession of the apartheid government of South Africa was to keep black men and white women away from one another. Similar to the situation in the United States, rumors of white women being harassed by black men in South Africa were met with swift retaliation by the government in the form of mass arrests and beatings.

This speech, given by South African president P. W. Botha on August 18, 1985, is quite telling:

> . . . Our Combat Unit is now training special white girls in the use of slow poisoning drugs. Ours is not a war where we can use the atomic bomb to destroy the Blacks, so we must use our intelligence to effect this. The person-to-person encounter can be very effective. As the records show that the black man is dying to go to bed with the white woman, here is our unique opportunity. . . . We have received a new supply of prostitutes from Europe and America. . . .*

Embracing the Image

Reverend Eugene Rivers's *Boston Review* article entitled "Beyond the Nationalism of Fools" noted that black scholars such as Cornel West, Henry Louis Gates, and others, while discussing Marx, Hegel, Foucault, and Derrida, must devote attention to the plight of black boys only a few miles from Harvard but representative of young black males around the country. He cites the following data:

A black male has a 1 in 3,700 chance of getting a Ph.D. in mathematics, engineering, or the natural sciences
A black male has a 1 in 766 chance of becoming an attorney
A black male has a 1 in 395 chance of becoming a physician

*Rumors persist among South African blacks that paid white prostitutes (some with AIDS) were widely used by the apartheid regime. They were literally advertised for after they had contracted AIDS in places such as Amsterdam, New York, and London, and imported to South Africa.

A black male has a 1 in 2 chance of not attending college,
    even if he graduates from high school

A black male has a 1 in 9 chance of using cocaine

A black male has a 1 in 12 chance of contracting gonor-
    rhea

A black male has a 1 in 20 chance of being imprisoned
    while in his twenties

These statistics are a sampling of data on the state of black males in America. It has been an important task for American policy makers to ensure that these data localize the "problems of black males" squarely on the shoulders of black men, rather than connecting the dots back to enslavement, failed social policies, and institutional racism. Social scientists are often reluctant to discuss how deeply rooted is the fear of black males in America and how this fear is related to white sexual insecurity. It is a taboo subject, with only a few persons daring to discuss it. Emerging as a recurrent theme in literature is the racist image of black people in the white psyche, particularly in the area of blacks' sensuality and their seeming "inability" to place intellect above bodily urges.

Consider the sources of the following quotations:

Among the blacks is misery enough, God knows, but no poetry. Love is the peculiar oestrum of the poet. Their love is ardent, but it kindles the senses only, not the imagination.

I think [a black] . . . could scarcely be found capable of tracing and comprehending the investigations of Euclid.

. . . in this country the slaves multiply as fast as the free inhabitants. Their situation and manners place the commerce between the two sexes almost without restraint . . . 567,614 inhabitants of every age, sex, and condition. But 296,852, the number of free inhabitants, are to 270,762, the number of slaves, nearly as 11 to 10. Under the mild treatment our slaves experience, and their wholesome, though coarse, food, this blot in our country increases as fast, or faster, than the whites.

—Thomas Jefferson, *Notes on the State of Virginia*, 1787

. . . the physical differences [which] will forever forbid the two races living together on terms of social and political equality. And inasmuch as they cannot so live while they do remain together there must be the position of superior and inferior, and I as much as any man am in favor of having the superior position assigned to the white race.

—Abraham Lincoln, 1864

"The Negro is primarily affectionate, immensely emotional, then sensual and under stimulation passionate . . . there is undeveloped artistic power and taste—Negroes make good artisans, handscraftsmen—and there is instability of character incident to lack of self-control, especially in connection with the sexual relation. . . ."

—Dr. Robert Bennett Bean, "Some Racial Peculiarities of the Negro Brain," *American Journal of Anatomy*, 1906

"[T]he mental constitution of the negro is . . . normally good-natured and cheerful, but subject to sudden fits of emotion and passion during which he is capable of performing acts of singular atrocity, impressionable, vain, but

often exhibiting in the capacity of servant a dog-like
fidelity which has stood the supreme test. . . . After
puberty sexual matters take the first place in the negro's
life and thoughts."

> —Entry under "Negro," *Encyclopaedia Britannica,* Volume 19,
> 1911

These quotations are representative of the literature—both
"scientific" and otherwise—that sought to instill a sense of inferiority in black people, and a sense of black people's "inferiority"
in whites. Indeed, the persistent theme of Western civilization
toward persons of color, blacks specifically, and black men in
particular, is that they are sensuous and unintelligent creatures
filled with unbridled lust. These assertions translated into public
policies encouraging the emigration of black Americans to Africa;
laws enforcing the separation of races, particularly of black men
and white women, and broad, tacit endorsement of violence
toward African Americans, particularly toward black men.

John Hope Franklin, in a stinging essay done for the nation's
bicentennial, argued that the "moral legacy of the Founding
Fathers" was the embedded racism stated explicitly in the Constitution and implicitly in the lives they led as slaveholders. The
ripple effect of this legacy led to the Civil War, lynching, and
enforced segregation that has been with us since the founding of
the nation. What is more damaging, however, is how these racist
views became the norm for how whites sexualized black men;
their subsequent fears then determined how black males could
be brutalized. Out of these attitudes would evolve an idealized
black male that was overtly desexualized and would take the
form of the watermelon-eating, slow-talking, and docile lackeys
such as those portrayed by Willie Best and Stepin Fetchit. His
opposite would be the "bad nigger," epitomized by the black-

faced whites in *The Birth of a Nation,* and more recently by some rap artists in music videos.

The Consequences of Adaptation

To deny that the barrage of negative stereotyping has not affected black male self-image is to ignore history and contemporary reality. Beginning with slavery, the need to survive forced many black men to adapt to white supremacist notions about themselves. This adaptation took many forms, such as engaging in little or no eye contact with more powerful white males and providing ego-boosting compliments to whites when they accomplished a minor feat. It is important to note that *not* recognizing the social cues provided by a white supremacist society in determining the status of black males could lead to premature death. My companions in the convenience store are the descendants of those who saw all black men as threats. Black men such as Emmett Till—more boy than man, actually—who did not recognize these cues were taught fatal lessons and used as examples for others who would transcend the unpredictable social barriers that were ever prevalent in Western society.

Imbibing the various identities assigned to them can be seen in the agony of Bert Williams as he performed in blackface during the early years of the twentieth century. It was seen in Mantan Moreland during the heyday of racism in Hollywood, and continued through the 1930s and 1940s with the tolerance of segregated entertainment in the Cotton Club and the "noble savage" characters portrayed by Sidney Poitier and Harry Belafonte in their earlier films.

After *Brown v. Board of Education* outlawed segregation in

public schools in the United States, the images mutated into forms that were even more bizarre. Self-hatred became even more fashionable than it already had been among black men as evidenced in how we "did" our hair. It took on complex rituals after Madame Walker's invention of the straightening comb. Malcolm X would analyze this in his autobiography as he "conked" his hair with lye to make it appear straight and more "white." It would continue with images of a bleached Michael Jackson and a blond Dennis Rodman, and reach its zenith with the racially unconscious lyrics of rappers such as 2 Live Crew and Too Short. What would be even more devastating is how the growing self-hatred among us would take the form of unprecedented violence between 1980 and 1995. Homicidal black-on-black violence reached an all-time high in 1993, with nearly two hundred black males (age eighteen to twenty-four) per one hundred thousand becoming victims, compared to only eighteen per one hundred thousand for white males during the same year. Some of the "halo effect" of the October 1995 Million Man March has been attributed to the recent dip in the homicide rate among young black males. Those who are less inclined to give Louis Farrakhan credit for the declining rate attribute it to the roaring economy that characterized the last half of the 1990s, although this belies the fact that homicide rates rose steadily and consistently beginning in 1984 and ignored economic upswings.

Perhaps the *greatest* indicator of self-hatred among black men is the two-thirds increase of suicide among black males age fifteen to twenty-four during the past fifteen years. Until 1980, black male suicide rates were some of the lowest in the nation, with suicide prevention programs viewing African-American men as extremely "low risk." The increase in suicide among black males is exacerbated by the notion of what I call "homisuicidal behavior"—self-destructive behavior in which one consciously takes unnecessary risks. It is found in the young black man who knowingly flirts with danger by driving into inner-city neighborhoods occupied by rival gangs and flashing gang signs, or in the young black men who drive at high rates of speed without wearing seat belts. The rate of death in this group of black males, age thirteen to nineteen, is nearly twice as high as for a comparable group of white males. Black people are half as likely to be buckled in as whites or Latinos, according to a national study in 1999 by Meharry Medical College and General Motors. "Death without seat belts" among black men gained national attention with the 2000 death of Kansas City linebacker Derrick Thomas, who was fatally injured in a car accident in which his companions were wearing seat belts and he was not.

2
How Black Boys Are Raised

Power is the ability to define reality and have other people respond to your definition as if it were their own.
—JAMAICAN PROVERB

Thomas

I was discussing with a friend of mine who is a father the problems his twelve-year-old son, Thomas, was having after his parents had enrolled him in a nearly all-white junior military academy. My friend said that Thomas hated the school and was being harassed by his classmates who called him "nigger" and "monkey." My friend and his wife are parents firmly ensconced in the black middle class, who have educated their oldest son and daughter in nearly all-white schools from K through 12.

"But Thomas needs to stay there, regardless of what they do to him," his father said to me, as if I had some control over their son's life at the school. "He'll be better able to get into West Point or any other college if he finishes _____ Academy.

"Are you concerned about the psychological damage that is being done to him?" I asked.

"That's a serious charge, and I don't believe that he's

undergoing any more pressure there than I faced when I was in school. He's got to learn to adjust to whatever is thrown at him from both blacks and whites."

"Have you talked to the headmaster and teachers at the school?" I asked, knowing that he probably had.

"Sure, that was one of the first things I did, and all of them agreed that the 'transition to a more diverse academy' might come at Tommy's expense."

"You know what I would do"? I asked, ready for opposition to the answer but feeling that my friend was arguing more with himself than with me.

"What?"

"I'd put him in a school where he wouldn't be exposed to such ridicule."

Without hesitation, my friend said, "You're right. I've known this for a long time; I just needed to hear it come from someone else. Why is it so hard to give black boys a good education without all the shit that white people throw on them?" Just like that.

The question my friend asked is the question that most black parents ask at least once during the education of their children. Black parents know that their sons are highly susceptible to circumstances, both unique and not, which render them vulnerable to racist institutions. Black parents possess few strategies, however, that can help them teach their boys how to successfully navigate through these labyrinthine organizations. This should not be interpreted as an indictment of black parenthood, but as an observation that African Americans, in general, and black parents, in particular, have a meager supply of social and educational strategies to protect their sons from a society that has a love-hate relationship with them.

I am still perplexed at how surprised we are when caught off guard by racism, both overt and covert. We know it exists because not only have we read about it, we've experienced it on a variety of levels and on a daily basis. Yet somehow we still view racism as an aberration rather than a consistent theme in American history. Even educated African Americans (and I use "African Americans" purposely here) seem shocked when a close encounter of the racial kind challenges the naive notion that they are somehow immune from it.

Tennessee State University—a historically black university located just a few miles from where I teach in Nashville—is just now discovering that its students were harassed while leaving football games by the security guards of Nashville's new stadium. That a group of black students should be synonymous with "gang presence" is not even the point, but that such harassment is commonplace because police *overpatrol* black adolescents, particularly in places such as Daytona Beach during spring break, or at the infamous Freaknik in Atlanta, during the mid-1990s.

I am alternately intrigued and confused by the calls I receive at my office from black parents and educators who are genuinely surprised that at the end of Du Bois's century of race such blatant discrimination is still so commonplace. They are genuinely confounded, fearful, and angry over the vulnerability of their children—particularly their sons—at something so "American" as a college football game. They want to believe that racism is dead, or at least on its deathbed, but, like the masked Jason, it continues to terrorize their children in the most unexpected places and at the most innocuous times.

"Transcending racism" for most African Americans, though viewed cynically by some, is part of the black American dream even though history proves that it will never happen. Derrick Bell's controversial thesis that racism is sewn permanently into the fabric of America is sobering and true. Critical race theorists in law such as Geneva Crenshaw provide compelling historical evidence that racism not only is here to stay, but that it mutates itself in ways that ensure its continued survival. African Americans naively remain faithful to strategies and practices that are "mainstream" and thought to be applicable to all people, but that can actually be quite detrimental to some.

One of those practices is child rearing. Very few people—black or white—follow books to the letter on how to raise their children. Instead, they choose to use the information to bolster their knowledge, whether it has been passed on to them or learned firsthand. Indeed, Benjamin Spock's *Baby and Child Care*, one of the best-selling books of all time, serves more as a *manual* rather than a treatise on what to do with children and what to expect at certain ages. It is consulted rather than followed, with the vast majority of parents simply doing what they think best when they raise their children.

Black people in moments of bitter irony can accuse one another—sometimes seriously, sometimes jokingly—of "acting white" or "not acting black enough." Thomas Parham, a noted black psychologist, uses the term *nigrescence* to describe stages of one's psychological identity as an African American. He discusses the Pre-Encounter Stage, during which a black person is oblivious to his/her identity as an African American, while those who incorporate African-American culture as essential to their psychological survival belong to the Immersion Stage of nigrescence. Such a model can be applied to black child rearing as well. From my experiences, and based on reams of sociological and psychological research, I believe there are three broad strategies for rearing black children in America: 1) the White Way, 2) the Gray Way, and 3) the Black Way.

Child-Rearing Strategies

The White Way

The White Way is practiced by most African Americans; it assumes that while society places undue burdens on young black men—police harassment, severe sentencing in juvenile courts, and low expectations for academic performance—it is basically "fair" to them, and if problems do arise, they can be solved within a system that is relatively stable and unbiased. If a black boy gets in trouble at school, it is assumed that, whatever the infraction, the appropriate discipline was meted out fairly and was in the context of the rules governing the school.

Parents who raise their sons in this way come from every class within the African-American community. While the method may be identified by the presence of child-rearing books such as Dr. Spock or reading *Parents* magazine in the home, it is also indicated by the total psychological submission of the parents to whatever "system" holds their son. There is little questioning about methods from these parents; in fact, the "system" may be defended, even if its treatment of the black boy is questionable.

I received a call not long ago from a single black mother whose son was complaining about taking Ritalin, a powerful drug that is given disproportionately to young black males. The drug is a stimulant and closely resembles the characteristics of cocaine. Taken orally, it can cause nausea, dizziness, headaches, and severe appetite loss. In 2000, the American Psychiatric Association (APA) was investigated for possible conspiracy with Ciba Geigy, the manufacturer of Ritalin, for exaggerating the frequency of Attention Deficit Disorder in order to share in the profit from the drug. By increasing the popularity of this "disorder," the APA increased sales of the drug. The primary takers of Ritalin have been boys, and among them it is highly prescribed to black boys.

Her son was prescribed the drug by a psychiatrist when the boy refused to come in from recess, which led to a schoolyard confrontation with his fifth-grade teacher. The boy told his mother that the drug made him "sleepy" (which she better described as "dizzy") and that he was tired of taking it. As a college professor, I had no authority to recommend that the drug be discontinued, but I suggested to the mother that she might want to get a second opinion from another psychiatrist as to whether this medication was necessary.

After a few moments of silence, the mother angrily asked if I *really* cared about her son. I replied that my commitment to the welfare of black children was absolute, and that my recommendation arose from that commitment. "Then how can you tell me not to have the very best drugs for my son?" she said. I told her that Ritalin is often recommended for black boys by educational systems more concerned about controlling them rather than educating them. "You mean to tell me that you think the teacher would recommend something that was not in the best interest of my son?" she asked sarcastically. I told her not only was that possible, but, again, that a trained physician familiar with Ritalin could verify this. In disbelief she said that her son should not have talked back to the teacher and that the teacher had a "right" to control him in any way she could. I paused and gently said that she should have a healthy skepticism about the commitment of any white-run school system that educated her children. Before the words were fully out of my mouth, she'd hung up. I replaced the phone in the cradle, hoping she would take my advice but knowing that she wouldn't.

Is she a "bad" mother? I don't think so. The very fact that she felt compelled to call me shows that she cares a great deal about the welfare of her son. She simply doesn't know how to place his well-being into context within the system to which she is adhering. Moreover, she is actually beholden to a system that has taught *her* that teachers are always right, that doctors know everything, and that schools educate children indiscriminately. She believes that the educational system actually cares about her son and that *he*, not the school, is the problem. Most black parents are convinced that their sons' schools are there to educate them because that is what they have been taught. Though they are more skeptical about the criminal justice system, they remain generally confident that schools are just and impartial in dealing with their sons. Again, this is not an indictment of black parenthood; in fact, it is a description of the misplaced faith that many of them unknowingly place in the institutions surrounding their sons. The White Way of child rearing is unreflective, not because parents of black boys are thoughtless or careless, but because they unconsciously *adjust* to racism's ubiquity and its impact on their children. Racism envelops persons completely and haunts like an unseen ghost in the homes, schools, and workplaces where African Americans live, learn, and work. Noted scholar Lewis Gordon writes in his book *Fanon and the Crisis of European Man* that

> With racism's permeation of daily life, grandiose assaults on racism—highly public spectacles against exceptional behavior—miss the mark. Racism, as a function of extraordinary individuals, conceals itself from itself through making its noxious values so familiar and frequent that they cease to function as objects of observation and reflection; they, in short, become unreflective and so steeped in familiarity that they become invisible.

Because I agree with Gordon, I always attempt to objectify to relatives and teachers of black boys the insidious and pernicious nature of white supremacy, and their unwitting acceptance of it within every area of their and their children's lives. I point out that educational curricula glorify the bravery of Patrick Henry but ignore the courage of Ida B. Wells-Barnett. Jefferson is seen as the great American intellectual yet W.E.B. Du Bois is barely discussed in most classrooms. "Classical music" means Bach, Mozart, and Haydn, and ignores the fact that *all* cultures have classical music, including African Americans, who have Scott Joplin, Duke Ellington, and John Coltrane. I challenge them to find one *black* author in *The Great Books of the Western World.*

The White Way is not the right way to rear black children and is not selected by black parents as much as it is *accepted,* because of a lack of choice and information and because of the omnipresent nature of racism in the lives of black folk. I know that black parents mean well, because I am a parent myself. We consult friends who offer us well-meaning advice that pertains to raising boys, not *black boys* specifically. We listen to psychologists, teachers, and other experts at parent-teacher meetings give insights on predictable stages of development for boys, *but not specifically black boys.* We browse bookstores and consult manuals that are not written with our boys in mind: boys who will grow up with the threat of police harassment, who are watched closely as they shop in department stores, who are disposed of more harshly by juvenile justice systems that refer to them as an "endangered species." We simply cannot all raise our sons the same, because black boys are different from white boys. Their legacy as African Americans marks them in ways that many whites simply don't or can't understand.

The Gray Way

The Gray Way of rearing black boys is characterized by parents' recognizing that the systems through which black boys travel must be carefully navigated. There is a healthy skepticism about criticism received from both black and white teachers, who may not have their sons' best interests at heart. Quite often, black parents who raise their sons by the Gray Way are viewed as troublemakers by the institutions that provide services for their children because they take time to review carefully both sides of any disciplinary issues. They usually make frequent visits to the school and write letters to those with authority over their children, challenging disciplinary action meted out to their sons.

The Gray Way is differentiated from the White Way by a *reaction* to racism rather than an unconscious *acceptance* of its presence. It understands that racism is part of the daily lives of black people in this country, and shuns solutions that seek to ignore cultural differences among children. Parents who rear their children in the Gray Way are often angry and frustrated at organizations and individuals that seem unrelenting in their denigration of black boys.

An educator and friend of mine recently told the story of how her then fifteen-year-old son was referred to by his white teacher as "Little Mr. Loser." Not surprisingly, her son was reluctant to go to school after his public humiliation in front of the class. After succeeding in pressing her son to reveal why he was hesitant about returning to his class, she headed straight for his school and angrily told his teacher never to refer to her son in that manner. The teacher sheepishly apologized, and a small victory was gained, only after the mother confronted a teacher who clearly knew a lot about hurting black children and little about nurturing them.

Parents raising their children in the Gray Way are skilled at challenging systems. They know how to organize, write letters, and protest. They may run into conflict with White Way parents who are hesitant at the notion that an institution may need to be challenged so that it ceases its discriminatory behavior toward black boys. They are good parents and spend time listening to their children with a "third ear," as Theodore Reik calls it, which tunes them in to what is happening to their sons. While often disappointed in the unrelenting racism that creates barriers for their sons, they are nonetheless prepared to deal with it, either individually or collectively. They also attempt to support White Way parents, which often proves futile since White Way parents may ridicule them for being too outspoken or simply "too black."

Many Gray Way parents are White Way parents who became convinced that the institutions through which their sons traverse are for white rather than black boys. Their evolution to Grayness comes from believing that institutions do not always do what is in the best interests of black children, particularly black boys. Their social evolution may stop at the Gray Way, or may continue until they begin rearing their sons the Black Way.

The Black Way

One day while volunteering to tell stories to young black children at a local elementary school, I noticed a six-year-old boy pushing a little girl in line in front of him. Scenes like this are repeated thousands of time in elementary schools, but this little girl was not going to put up with it and shoved right back. When I walked over to provide some fatherly discipline, the little boy, clearly frustrated that she was neither impressed nor intimidated by his bullying, called her a "ho." I was shocked to hear the word coming from his six-year-old lips but, sadly, not surprised. He saw me right after he said it, and looked sheepishly down at the floor. I asked him where he'd heard the word, and he quietly answered "TV." "What does it mean?" I asked; he answered that it was a "girl who did something bad." I told him to apologize, and he did, turning only slightly to the frowning young lady who had now crossed her little arms and was glaring at him. I then motioned for him to follow me out of the line and into a corner, where I spent the next twenty minutes giving him simple lessons in courtesy.

About a half hour later, my new little friend, who was by now telling me the things six-year-olds tell adults, asked if he could sit on my lap during storytime. I told him yes, since I was at the school being a "role model" for the children. He then looked at me quizzically and asked in the sincerest of voices, "You my daddy?" I was touched by this simple question. I quietly answered that I was like a father to him, as well as to all the other children there. This was all he needed to hear, and he instantly announced to his friends gathering at the table "He my daddy!" and although they laughed, they did not dispute his claim. He then hugged me tightly, and we began to read a story together.

I thought it telling that this child, who was now seeking fatherly acceptance and guidance, had only a moment before been acting out what he'd come to believe—even at his tender age—was his role in regards to his young sister. A victim of various media's pernicious affect on young black boys, this six-year-old boy was already adept in how to denigrate girls. By the time he grows to adulthood, he'll be even better skilled at disrespecting black women. The way we raise our black boys in America has been a poor imitation of the way white boys are raised. Those who raise black boys are, with few exceptions, ignoring the impact of racism on our children and are casual about teaching black boys the importance of understanding and respecting other African Americans. Black Way parents are rare. At the core of their child-rearing methods is the belief that African-centered methods and values are the *only* choice in raising healthy black boys in America. The celebration of African culture is reflected in their homes with artwork, books, and memorabilia reflecting a love of Africa. Kwanzaa is given a place in their homes, and its *Nguzo Saba* (Seven Principles) are valued throughout the year and taught to future generations.

These parents see their sons as warriors doing battle on several levels with racism, and they support them in these struggles. While their sons may go to traditionally white institutions for education or recreation, they believe that, at best, these institutions can *train* their children but not *educate* them. They believe their children's education is the direct responsibility of parents and relatives, and they know that their children's education goes far beyond the four walls of a school. They see black institutions such as African-centered churches, museums, and universities as bastions against traditional methods of learning, and place their sons in environments where they can learn about self as well as things.

Similar to Gray Way parents, Black Way parents find protest a necessary tool to ensure that their sons will receive proper treatment in whatever organization they find membership. Their protest, however, is made with the idea of *systemic* change that will challenge the very essence of the organization. These changes can take the form of creating an alternative school, college, or recreational group that is more culturally specific to African ideals. The education of their children is viewed as belonging to the parents and not the school system, and care is taken in who educates their children as well as where they are educated. When their sons reach university level, historically black colleges and universities are high on their list; even if the final college selection is a traditionally white institution, their sons are carefully guided and counseled on the major selection with regard to professors' attitudes toward black boys.

Black Way parents tirelessly recruit from the ranks of White Way and Gray Way parents, by introducing to them to African-centered values in the form of institutions, books, celebrations, dress, and food. They may invite other parents to the increasingly popular "rites of passage" ceremonies for black boys, which induct them into manhood. Black Way parents focus on institutional change and, again, while protest is in their repertoire, it is viewed as a means to an end rather than an end in itself. They see an African inside of every "Negro," and they encourage his emergence in conversation. They believe that the adoption of African-centered values is transformational and not just a ceremonial exercise employing African clothing and hairstyles. The transformation goes far deeper into cherishing values that reflect the strength and courage of long-forgotten ancestors who triumphed in the face of adversity.

The Warrior Method of Raising Black Boys

I chose colors to introduce these three ways of raising black males in order to create a visual image of how racism impacts upon the rearing of our children. The "Black Way," however, is better referred to as the Warrior Method, since it implies that those who are serious about the healthy passage of black males from boyhood to manhood must *fight* to accomplish this. I use the word *fight* because it is exactly that.

Educators of black boys, whatever their race, if dedicated to the unpopular proposition that they wish to have a healthy, safe, and relaxed environment for black boys, will be challenged in their efforts to accomplish this. Teachers who adopt the Warrior Method often run headlong into trouble at the schools in which they teach. In October 1999, Yaa Asantewa Nzingha, a middle school teacher in Brooklyn, was absent from her drama class for one day. Richard Levine taught the twenty-five-year veteran schoolteacher's class in her absence and asked her students to do some improvisational acting. He asked one of the students to pretend that he was stealing something as a way of impressing girls. The student said no because "all black people don't steal." When Levine asked the young Kurtis Lee who taught him that, Lee responded, "Ms. Nzingha teaches us that as Africans we shouldn't fall into the standards of America." Nzingha was placed under investigation for telling her students that they are *not* Americans but Africans. Efforts were made to suspend this teacher, who has won extraordinary praise from the very system that investigated her, and to revoke her New York teaching license as well. Her African-centered curriculum, taught at a school that supposedly encourages individual expression, runs squarely in the face of administrators who are resentful toward Warrior Method teachers who want the best for their students. In late 2000, she was fired from the Brooklyn, New York, school system.

White persons in particular will be queried closely about why they are "going to the mats" for a black male in ways that are subtly racist. This may seem harsh, but many well-meaning whites view working with black boys as "missionary work." Black boys do not need saviors, they need advocates who will aid in their healthy development. The popular theme of white people saving black males is portrayed in such films as *Sunset Park,* *Dangerous Minds* (an interesting title) and *Class Act.* Hollywood enjoys the plot of white persons rescuing black people from a host of evils, perhaps as a way of obtaining absolution from past evils toward them. They may be viewed by other whites as a "traitor" to the idea that black boys are part of a throwaway generation, who do not deserve the attention they receive from their white intercessors. Author Tim Wise, a white male who is a thorn in the side of white supremacists like David Duke, calls these people "race traitors" since they betray their white neutrality toward racial matters. Dedicated whites such as Wise are rare, however, and people like him, John Brown, the militant antebellum white abolitionist, and others are examples of the inevitable ostracism that whites encounter when they aggressively fight against racism.

Black intercessors willing to adopt the Warrior Method will also face stiff opposition as they defy systems and procedures that hurt black boys. They may force a school system to enhance the celebration of Black History Month, agitate for the inclusion of black heroes and sheroes on the walls gazed upon by young black males who rarely see blacks in positive adult roles. The Warrior Method calls for a vigilance toward media, schools, churches, and social-service agencies that serve black boys. The Warrior Method provides appropriate reading lists, has ready a set of lawyers who argue for justice under the law, and is aware of cultural events that will enhance the self-esteem of black boys. This method calls for a full-time commitment to do battle with systems that are oblivious to the needs of black boys. The Warrior method is not a battle that will be enjoined only by black people, but by anyone serious about eliminating social barriers that block the paths toward healthy development in young black boys.

Very few people have a clear understanding of the challenges faced by black boys as they mature. We already know that there is denial in America about the entrenched nature of racism, as evidenced in the 1997 Gallup poll. The survey showed an ever-widening gulf between blacks and whites on a number of social issues that range from affirmative action to the presence of racial prejudice and job opportunity. These differences are increasing rather than decreasing, and they destroy the notion that in times of prosperity racism will disappear like dew when met with the sun's rays. If dedicated people who raise, teach, work with, and volunteer for black boys are up to these challenges, they will commit in tangible ways to the children they work with. Magical solutions that many parents and educators are looking for when working with black males don't exist. There are no easy ways to counter the assaults aimed at black boys. The ten points that follow are what I consider essential in beginning an effective intervention with black boys. They come from listening to parents and educators over many years as well as putting them into practice in my own teaching.

The Ten Commitments of the Warrior Method

1. *Maintain a strong commitment to educating black boys.* Too often just lip service is paid to working with black boys. Rather, consultants should be brought in to give workshops and provide recommendations for challenges facing educators and human service workers. Educators who claim they want the best for black boys should know about them, read about them, play with them, and, most of all, intervene on their behalf if they are unjustly punished for minor infractions.

2. *Possess a deep and abiding knowledge of global black history.* No parent or educator of children should be unaware of the history of the children they teach. The Kenyan proverb,

"Until lions have historians, hunters will be heroes," is important when educating black boys; it emphasizes the importance of reversing perspectives in telling the history of black people. I have seen the eyes of black children light up when they hear about Nzingah's courage against the Portuguese, Wells-Barnett's commitment to justice, and Denmark Vesey's dedication to freedom. A committed educator will use these stories to help black boys locate themselves psychologically in the river of black history. See Appendix A for an annotated bibliography about black history.

The idea of Africans in the *Maafa* possessing an African-centered worldview did not begin with the Afrocentric movement in the mid-1970s. It has been a consistent theme throughout the writings of black people in all parts of the world. In this country, Maria Stewart (1803–1879) of Boston, the first African-American woman to publish her speeches, refused to let anyone address her as other than "an African." Throughout her life she remained outspoken about the "need of Africans to build their own schools and stores." Her book, *Meditations from the Pen of Mrs. Maria Stewart* was written totally from the perspective of being an African in America rather than an "African American." Likewise, David Walker's (1785–1830) *Appeal to the Colored Citizens of the World,* written in 1829, called for self-defense among all enslaved Africans and stated that "it is no more harm for you to kill the man who is trying to kill you than it is for you to take a drink of water." Martin Delany (1812–1885), a physician and the highest-ranking black person in the Union Army, signed a contract with the Nigerian government in 1859 that allowed for cotton production by free West Africans and serious negotiations to repatriate all Africans in the *Maafa* back to their Motherland.

Such calls for an African-centered consciousness persisted in this country during the twentieth century with the Harlem Renaissance and abroad during the 1920s with the *Négritude* movement and West Africans such as Aime Césaire, Leon Dumas, and Leopold Senghor. Perhaps the greatest manifestation of this African-centered consciousness was the efforts of Marcus Garvey's Back to Africa movement, which mobilized millions of Africans in the United States, the Caribbean, and Europe to look toward Africa as a place for freedom and true liberation. His influence can be found in the writings of Elijah Muhammad (1897–1975) of the Nation of Islam. W.E.B. Du Bois (1864–1963), the "father of pan-Africanism," would also discuss the importance of being an African, would spend his last years in Ghana and eventually die and be buried there. Audley Moore (1898–1997), better known as "Queen Mother Moore," would become one of the greatest proponents of African-centered education of this century and would consistently be listed with Elijah Muhammad and Marcus Garvey as one of the greatest organizers of African Americans during the twentieth century.

3. *Read at least thirty minutes a day on African/African-American culture and life.* Similar to the second commitment, the dedicated mentors to black boys will learn more about the culture from which they emerge. They will read books and magazines that will teach them about what black boys are seeing, hearing, and talking about. I am surprised about how little black parents know about hip-hop culture, thereby cutting off an avenue of communication with their sons. Asking a black boy what he learned in school will get far less attention than asking him if he has heard a particular Dead Prez album. Parents and educators, without using gimmicks,

should use "bridges" to reach the black boys with whom they are familiar. Communicating with black boys about their thoughts, music, and heroes begins the process of socializing them in productive ways.

4. *Be comfortable in predominantly black environments.* I always ask white teachers if they feel comfortable in black churches, universities, and other social settings where they are a minority. Many white people find it difficult to exist in such surroundings since they may feel more comfortable controlling their environment than learning from it. A preacher friend of mine says, "White people don't make good minorities." Funny though this may be, the truth is that most white people spend very little time immersed in black sur- roundings. The converse is true, and black people are encouraged to "adjust" to their predominantly white settings, be it a school, the workplace, or the location of leisure-time activity. It is not uncommon for black parents to tell me that they chose to send their children to a predominantly white college so that they "can get used to dealing with white folks," as if this would not happen as a matter of course as their chil- dren mature. Most whites, however, are not prepared for pre- dominantly black environments; they actually go out of their way to avoid them. Those interested in adopting the Warrior Method in raising or teaching black boys must acknowledge and lose such inhibitions if they wish to operate sincerely in their interactions with them.

5. *Attend African-centered religious institutions.* The faith com- munity remains a powerful influence in black communities. It serves as an excellent bridge for helping the spiritual growth of African-American boys, and is a place for organizing around

issues affecting them. I am impressed with teachers who participate in black spiritual gatherings and are aware of how black churches can help in working with black boys.

6. *Volunteer at least five hours a month in a human service activity that engages black boys.* The emphasis here again is to know the environments in which black boys learn and play. Volunteering is an indication of commitment to addressing the needs of black boys. Serving as a teacher's aide, coaching basketball, and attending meetings at Boys and Girls Clubs can give volunteers a more comprehensive view of black boys' lives in America.

7. *Understand all bureaucracies that impact black boys.* This is a major task but necessary in committing to working with and raising black boys. I encourage parents, teachers, and volunteers who work with black boys to know who serves on the governing boards of institutions they attend, and who directs, administers, and otherwise runs the organizations. They should be familiar with the annual reports, should discuss "insider information" about the diversity of the administrators on the board, and should know who funds the organization and how much is being donated to it. Who is the chief of police? Who is the clerk in the juvenile court? Who makes up the health care organizations that are sensitive to pediatric care of black boys? Information of this nature should be readily available to persons interested in black boys in case strategic protest becomes necessary in advocating for them.

8. *Organize against environments oppressive of black boys.* Those committed to ensuring the healthy development of black boys should be prepared to intervene politically on

their behalf. Protest against policies or individuals who exercise discriminatory behavior toward black boys should be a tactic in the arsenal of those who adopt the Warrior Method of raising them.

9. *Read the following five books:*

Beloved by Toni Morrison—The greatest African-American love story ever told. It details the emotional impact of slavery on Africans in America. Based on the true story of Margaret Garner, who, in 1856, slashed the throat of one of her children rather than have them returned to slavery, the book tells about the impact of enslavement on the relationships between black women and men.

Yurugu by Marimba Ani—Perhaps the most comprehensive African-centered critique of European systems of thought ever written. Ani makes the necessary connections between how European systems by design support discriminatory behavior toward people of color.

The Miseducation of the Negro by Carter G. Woodson—The classic book offered by the "father" of African-American history, on why blacks *and* whites have been miseducated. Written nearly seventy years ago, it gives the reader a comprehensive view of how to educate black people.

There Is a River by Vincent Harding—Harding takes the reader from Africa to the Civil War, from the *point of view* of being African in America. The shift in perspective makes African Americans the *subject* rather than the *object* of historical analysis.

The Art of War by Sun Tzu—Written nearly twenty-four hundred years ago, it is the oldest book on strategizing against intractable systems. A must-read for those working with black boys and the bureaucracies they face.

10. *Teach at least two other persons each month about the Ten Commitments.* At every opportunity, educators and parents should provide counterpoints to the negative stereotyping of black boys. Discussing these commitments is a small but necessary step in dismantling these stereotypes.

The Ten Commitments are tough assignments, but successfully raising black boys in a racist society is a difficult job. I know, because I am constantly bombarded with questions from the private, public, and educational sectors on how to raise/teach/educate/entertain/discipline/talk to/impress/cajole/understand black boys by persons who, though sincere, are looking for a quick fix that simply does not exist. Questions are rarely asked about the "challenges of raising white girls." White boys, until recently, were thought to be fairly well integrated into "mainstream" America. Witness the orgies in Daytona Beach during spring break: higher levels of anxiety were raised in response to the black gatherings than to the white gatherings even though both were far less destructive than what has occurred in that city for years. "Boys will be boys" may be more accurately stated as "white boys will be white boys"; black boys don't "enjoy the privilege" of raucous behavior to the same extent as their white counterparts.

Saul Alinsky, one of the greatest community organizers of all time, said, "Change means movement. Movement means friction. Only in the frictionless vacuum of a nonexistent abstract world can movement or change occur without that abrasive friction of conflict." Black boys live in a world that has strong and misguided opinions about them, based on centuries of misinformation. It will take sometimes abrasive strategies to effect the changes necessary to guarantee them a fair chance at life. Those who are committed to them need to be prepared with strategies that include both negotiation *and* confrontation.

3
Necessary Tools for African Warriors

The present system under the control of the whites trains the Negro to be white and at the same time convinces him of the impropriety of the impossibility of his becoming white. It compels the Negro to become a good Negro for the performance of which his education is ill-suited.

—CARTER G. WOODSON

NWA

I was waiting in the cluttered office of the diminutive-looking white teacher, observing the drawings and desk that most middle school teachers have. Her disheveled appearance matched her office, and I glanced at a small plant that was begging to be watered on a bookshelf. The shelf was populated with volumes about inner-city life with yellow stickies protruding from them. The teacher had asked me months earlier to speak to her class— a group of about fifteen black boys, who for one reason or another had failed to learn the school curriculum. She was now down the corridor on "hall duty," monitoring the students to make sure they got to their classes without incident. I took the moment alone to glimpse at the memorabilia teachers display when their students do well on their assignments. There were holiday essays about the self-effacing pilgrims, Columbus's meanderings throughout the West Indies, and the greatness of Washington and Jefferson. Not one symbol in the teacher's office was culturally specific to the children she was assigned to teach. As I continued my visual tour of her office, I was interrupted by her entering the room and apologizing for making me wait. Out of breath and clearly frazzled, she began to describe the students to whom I was about to speak. They were "very unruly," she said, and had a near total disregard for "authority." She gave me an advanced apology for their behavior and said that she saw the importance of "black men as role models for young black boys," and that this was her motivation in asking me to speak to them during Black History Month.

I nodded my head, having been part of this scene so many times. I'd even mused on the idea of creating a for-profit agency dubbed Rent a Middle-class Brother for your Organization (RAMBO); requests for such engagements are very frequent and involve black men from the business, educational, and government sectors. The teacher was rambling on distractedly about how all the boys "defied" authority and how she simply had "no idea" about how to "control them." I was sure that I would talk to them about self-esteem; how I would begin I did not know, but I was eager to get started and steered her to the door. Before entering the classroom, she gave me one last apologetic look, as if she were leading me before a firing squad.

The chaotic class was filled with about fifteen black boys between the ages of twelve and fourteen who were engaged in everything from cursing to playing cards. Two sat in the back completely zoned out, the music from their earphones audible over the din. The others, talking loudly about girls and other things, totally disregarded our presence. Their teacher almost crept into the room ahead of me. Once inside she asked everyone to take a seat "because there was a guest speaker." Several of the boys continued talking as they slowly complied with her directions and sat down. We both knew that her waiting for absolute silence would be a waste of time, so she began *reading* the introduction I had provided her with while the boys continued their discussion about things more important to them. In fact, their voices grew louder as she droned on.

When she said my name, signaling the end of her soliloquy, I got up in front of the class and said good morning. A few replied, but most were indifferent or simply ignored me altogether. On impulse, I turned to the blackboard and wrote in the largest letters possible "NWA." I then asked what the letters stood for, and nearly all the boys said, "Niggas with Attitude." I had done the first thing that any teacher needs to do: get the students' attention. I next asked them why a group of young black men would call themselves "niggas." Nearly all the boys replied that it was a term of endearment and that it was not negative unless a *white* person called them that. I told them that I thought it was negative, and they all disagreed. I had done the second thing that a teacher needed to do: engage them in a dialogue.

I then asked how many of them cared if I called them "nigga." When no one replied, I said that for the next ten minutes I would do exactly that. They laughed and challenged me to go ahead. I started asking them questions about what words like *self-esteem*, *success*, and *challenges* meant, and I made sure that, regardless of who answered my question, I would preface it by saying, "Yes, Nigga" when I called on him. I continued to call them "nigga" throughout each exchange, and ended by saying, "Thanks, Nigga." After about five minutes, it was clear that I was causing unease with my casual use of the word. Their laughter had long faded, and the boys were becoming agitated and angry.

Suddenly, one of the students raised his hand; after I

acknowledged him by saying, "Yes, Nigga," he replied that he did not like my calling him that. I asked why, and he said that it sounded different the way I was using it. I asked how, and he said it just didn't sound the same and that it seemed so ugly now that I had drawn his attention to it. His classmates nodded in agreement. I thanked him without calling him a "nigga," then explained what the words *objectification* and *brainwashing* meant. The third and most important task of a teacher had taken place: the students had rolled an idea around in their heads, considered it, and *learned* something.

I launched into a brief discussion about how black people could remake different words that reflected self-esteem, as had occurred with *black* during the 1960s and *African* during the 1990s. I went on to explain that the word *Nigga* was only *rented* and not *owned* by us, and that was the reason why we felt it was a term that only we could use to describe ourselves or one another. One of the boys asked me if a white person had ever called me a "nigga." I said yes, several times, and that the time I remembered most was from when I was twelve and was feeding my dogs in the backyard of our Hough Avenue house in Cleveland. Some southern white men, who had managed to come north and were camping in the parking lot of a soon-to-be-all-black bar named Jo-Lu's, next door to where we lived, called me a "nigger" for no other reason than intimidation. I said nothing, fed my dogs, went inside, and told my father what had happened. Without even getting the details, he went down in the basement, retrieved a baseball bat, and told me to come with him. I obeyed and walked into the backyard with him. When he saw the men, he asked me which one called me that. I pointed to him. By this time the displaced southerners started backing up even though they outnumbered my father six to one. He ran toward the man who was halfway up a chain-link fence that bordered the yard.

The other men scattered, and my father told the one on the fence that if he ever saw him again he would "kick his ass." I felt good. So did the boys in the classroom. They were listening to my story with rapt attention, and I ended by telling them it was important for black fathers to protect their sons.

For the next thirty minutes, learning took place in the classroom. We talked about the importance of education and knowledge of black culture and history. We discussed the importance of reading something every day about black people's contribution to world culture and American society. We talked about the importance of educating other black boys about how society hurts them both physically and psychologically. We finished by discussing the need for excellence in whatever they did as black boys. I then told them that they were young warriors in a battle to retain and understand who they are as young black people and that they must never compromise the part of them that was African. I listened and became overwhelmed by how all of these handsome young black boys were eager to learn, eager to contribute, but were understimulated by a learning environment that was both sociologically and historically irrelevant and oftentimes boring. I glanced at their frightened teacher, who wore a look of pure amazement on her face at how curious and articulate her students could be.

I finished the discussion by passing out my business card—something that all the boys wanted—and told them if they wrote (not called) me, I would send them a book about black people. They agreed to do so, and after thanking them and telling them to stay strong, I ended my discussion. They clapped, cheered, and asked me when I would be back again. I told them as soon as their teacher invited me.

As the teacher and I walked out of the classroom and back toward her office, she marveled at what had just occurred. She said that she "could never do that," and I agreed with her. She told me that she simply could not get their attention in the manner I had used, and I again agreed with her. She stopped outside of her office, looked me dead in the eye, and told me that perhaps she needed to stop teaching in the inner city because what she had learned in graduate school seemed totally irrelevant to her students. I agreed with her and told her that if she were unwilling to submit to a complete overhaul of what was necessary to teach black boys, she should quit and teach white children. She was not offended by this suggestion and actually seemed relieved that I was relating to her so frankly about black boys. I left her, and during the next three months sent eight books to the boys in her class.

I walked into the class that day with no idea as to what I was going to tell those boys. I knew that my message would be about how they should be warriors, but I didn't know how I was going to get there. Though it is an unpopular idea among educators to include spirituality in teaching, I think it is important to understand the African ancestral spirit that follows those who teach young blacks. On that particular day, I believe that the ancestors provided me with a relevant example that would capture the attention of the boys. I needed their attention, and the use of an illustration that was culturally relevant to them was important.

Raising boys to be African warriors requires a dedication beyond what most educators are willing to give and beyond what many parents are capable of; since it goes far beyond what many of them *want* to do. It takes searching for a history that has been lost, and then setting up venues where this history can be taught. Because traditional educational settings are resistant to helping children who have been designated as "special," "disruptive," and "incorrigible," Saturday mornings may have to be sacrificed to do this. Likewise, parents and guardians of black boys will have to begin an avid reading program with their sons and learn about youth culture—something that parents may not wish to do. As an educator, I believe that most, but not all, parents want their children to learn. But many are unwilling to provide supplemental black education and rely solely on schools to teach their children. Educating young warriors entails going far beyond traditional methods of teaching. Urie Treisman's research at Berkeley did wonders in teaching young black children calculus and other mathematics long after schools had given up on them. Teachers such as Marva Collins who defy systems and who have a vision for their students, unaffected by what is said about them, have characterized the history of successful educational strategies for black children. In the early 1970s, she fought tooth and nail before she decided to break away from the Chicago public school system to establish West Side Preparatory in 1975. I have taught graduates of West Side Prep; they are some of the most brilliant black students I've met, and several of them are now earning advanced degrees in a host of fields.

Educators, both black and white, are usually punished for providing pedagogical innovations outside of what is required by the school district. Indeed, the history of educating African-American children about who they are is a history of struggle. Teaching Africans in America to read was illegal in most southern states and could result in death during the period of enslavement. Laurence Clifton Jones's 1909 establishment of Piney Woods Country Life School outside of Jackson, Mississippi, was done with great risk to his life and to the lives of his students.

Carter G. Woodson's scathing indictment on how African Americans are *miseducated* reads like yesterday's newspaper. Woodson focuses nearly his entire critique on the issue of *control* of what black children learn. The twentieth century is peppered with accounts of the resistance to educating black children, including the integration of public schools following *Brown v. Board of Education*. It continues with the resistance encountered by those who advocate African-centered education for black children, particularly black boys.

Lawsuits were filed against Malcolm X Academy in Detroit for being an all-boys school and teaching an African-centered curriculum, despite the fact that the grades and standardized test scores were significantly higher than those of comparable boys in mixed classes. The Baseline Essays introduced into the Portland, Oregon, public school system in the 1980s were roundly criticized for their content. The fact that attendance and test scores were significantly higher than those of black children in traditional classes was ignored, yet no alternative curriculum was offered by "anti-Afrocentrists" decrying the "unscientific" nature of the essays. Dinesh D'Souza, like so many others critical of African-centered educational methods, seems more concerned with hegemonic control over curricula than innovative methods for teaching black children. This is particularly true of the young black male, the icon of poor educational achievement.

At the higher-education level, African-centered education has met resistance primarily by conservative white educators such as Arthur Schlesinger and Mary Lefkowitz. Lefkowitz's book *Not Out of Africa: How Afrocentrism Became an Excuse to Teach Myth as History* was a full-frontal attack on the teachings of such educators as John Henrik Clarke, Molefi Asante, and Marimba Ani. Lefkowitz's disingenuous attempt to portray Afrocentricity as an educational plague visited upon innocent black children is not so much an attack on the theory as it is a defense against what she sees as a denigration of Western literature, history, and science. Arthur Schlesinger sees, in near apocalyptic terms, Afrocentricity as a direct attack against Western knowledge, particularly as it relates to what black children need to know. Black academics, too, have contributed their voices to criticizing African-centered approaches to higher education. Henry Louis "Skip" Gates, chair of Harvard's Black Studies Department, has been referred to by the *Chronicle of Higher Education* as the "Booker T. Washington of Black Studies," a not-so-subtle reference to his ability to define the field of Black Studies the way Washington defined education for black people over a century ago. Gates's influence is viewed by serious African-centered scholars as unduly conservative and, in many cases, misleading as to the importance of African-centered worldviews. The firestorm that arose after his 1999 PBS special, *Wonders of the African World*, centered on its condescending portrayal of Africa and its people. Pejoratively referred to as "Skip's World" and "Blunderer in the African World" by some, the PBS travelogue was thoroughly criticized by African scholars who saw it as total distortion of Africa and its people. The recent publication of Gates and Anthony Appiah's *Africana*, portrayed by them as a "fulfillment" of W.E.B. Du Bois's dream of an "Encyclopaedia Africana," is far from being such, and has also been met with criticism. Many inaccuracies plague the first edition, which, ironically, does not even contain an entry for the word *Africa*!

It seems hypocritical that as long as black children receive overdoses of white culture in nearly all of their subjects, no attention was paid on how such knowledge generally failed to raise test scores or appreciably diminish school absenteeism. Yet when black educators achieve these two modest but necessary behaviors for learning, they are criticized for creating "myths" about human history and science. Forget that George Washington never took an ax to a cherry tree, threw a dollar over the Delaware, or stood up in a rowboat to get across that same river. Forget about the racism that pervaded American presidents from Washington through Eisenhower, as documented by Kenneth O'Reilly in *Nixon's Piano*. As Maulana Karenga has noted, much of Western history is self-congratulatory and full of myths that reinforce the notion of white superiority and black inferiority. Teaching black boys to understand their own history and its relationship to white supremacist history is an essential characteristic of educating them.

The Four Cs

The Ten Commitments are essential characteristics needed by those raising and teaching black boys. They should be the impetus for achieving four goals in the healthy development of young black men. These "Four Cs"—consciousness, commitment, cooperation, and community—summarize what I have learned from more than a quarter of a century of teaching and discovering what really works when educating black youth.

Consciousness

Black consciousness is being aware of who you are as an African in the *Maafa,* realizing how you came to be in your present condition, and using that knowledge to understand your future. It is imbibing African culture at numerous levels in one's life and reflecting it in work and play.

I begin all of my classes at Fisk University by asking my students, "Who are you?" The most common reply is that they are male, female, a freshman, a sophomore, an Alpha Kappa Alpha, or something else. It is rare that within the first two or three responses the students describe themselves as "African" or an

"African in America." One may say that the absence of such descriptors merely proves how far removed the average black person is from their "African roots." I would agree with that and add simply that it is precisely this distance from their African selves that prevents them from learning effectively. Psychologist Na'im Akbar says that four disordered personalities arise from African Americans who imbibe heavily of European culture at the expense of connecting with their African selves:

Alien-Self Disorders—"These are the growing number of African Americans in recent years who have been socialized in families with primarily materialistic goals. They see themselves as material and evaluate their worth by the prevalence of material accouterments which they possess. . . ." Akbar says that the alien-self disorder is increasingly prevalent among professional African Americans who seek to imitate the dominant culture of the United States. Known as "Afro-Saxons" among many, sociologist Nathan Hare calls them the "black Anglo-Saxons" because of their absorption of white middle-class culture and its accompanying disorders.

Anti-Self Disorders—This disorder is characterized by a near complete identification with the dominant American culture. They exhibit hostility toward other African Americans, and may work actively against them if they are in a position of authority within white America. Viewed by whites as a "good Negro," these African Americans are Super Slaves to a culture that rewards them for opposing their African American cultural roots. They are the exact opposite of Norman Mailer's idea of the "White Negro" and seek approval from whites, which may even be manifested in marrying members of the group.

Self-Destructive Disorders—Oppression creates environments where individuals destroy themselves. These conditions can lead to homicidal violence; those on the outside may see drug dealing, prostitution, and pimping as "natural" for the group. Lacking consciousness of self leads to self-destructive behavior in a culture that encourages deracinated people. African Americans who fit this description are not necessarily poor and unemployed; indeed, they can be wealthy and famous but prone to behavior that demonstrates low self-esteem and the tendency toward taking risks. Their identity is viewed as antithetical to "mainstream" Eurocentric values, and they are usually feared by the dominant society because of their antisocial behavior.

Organic Disorders—Pollution, lead-based paint, and other environmental factors can lead to disorders that stunt the healthy growth of black boys. According to the National Institute of Allergy and Infectious Diseases, African Americans were three to four times more likely than whites to be hospitalized for asthma, and were four to six times more likely to die from it. "Poverty, substandard housing that results in increased exposure to certain indoor allergens, lack of education, inadequate access to health care, and the failure to take appropriate medications may all contribute to the risk of having a severe asthma attack or, more tragically, of dying from asthma." Man-made substances such as lead, asbestos, and airborne carcinogens can breed mental retardation, asthma, and higher rates of cancer in African-American children and can subsidize the psychological damage done to many black boys at young ages.

These disorders arise naturally from an environment that does not reinforce the healthy development of black identity in young African-American boys. Implicit in white curricula are books, films, and other learning materials that buttress the notion that being white is something positive and contributes to the general well-being of the planet. This "white consciousness" is not even objectified, so it makes it nearly impossible to have a discussion about it. "Being white" means being "American," a good citizen, and a human being, while "being black" implies the Du Boisian notion of "twoness" and alienation. In *Souls of Black Folk*, Du Bois said: "One ever feels his twoness—an American, a Negro; two souls, two thoughts, two unreconciled strivings; two warring ideals in one dark body, whose dogged strength alone keeps it from being torn asunder."

I believe that Du Bois's "twoness" does reside in many, but not all, African Americans. Raising a black child does not necessarily mean that he or she will be confused about his or her racial identity. This phrase from Du Bois is often quoted to indicate that at best African Americans will grow up confused about who they are. An early commitment to raising black consciousness and secure African-American children will guarantee that they will grow up without a divided racial identity.

Consciousness is the first and most fundamental step in raising healthy black boys in America. A consciousness of how one "fits" into the *Maafa* and a world reeling from racism allow young black boys to see themselves in a far broader context than what is taught to them in schools. For educators to reconnect the links between young Africans in America and their ancestors is important. The beginning of this can take the form of reading stories of ancient Africa aloud to preschool black boys. Finding suitable books is much easier than it was even ten years ago; the availability of African-centered materials has grown considerably. Here are some steps that can be taken to build a consciousness of the African self among African-American boys:

Begin at young ages to read aloud to boys about African Americans heroes and sheroes. Child psychologist Bruno Bettelheim says that the four most beautiful words in a child's ear are "Once upon a time." I agree, and these words can introduce black boys to the fascinating history of Africans in the *Maafa*. Reading aloud to black boys creates an early love of imagination and understanding of the world they live in and their place within it.

Insist that school systems recognize various cultural holidays in schools that are relevant to Africans in the **Maafa**. The most celebrated holiday devoted to African-American history is Martin Luther King Jr.'s birthday. In many areas, its celebration remains controversial, with some school systems grumbling about its "intrusion" on the academic calendar. Black History Month follows close behind, with some schools mounting sophisticated programs that celebrate the history of black people.

This is as it should be, and parents can suggest to schools other notable days such as Malcolm X's birthday on May 19, pre-Kwanzaa celebrations, and other events that detail the history of African Americans. School calendars in general should celebrate a variety of ethnic holidays pertaining to all persons. I am amused when I see nearly all-black elementary schools asking their students to wear green on St. Patrick's Day when virtually none of the students have any ancestral connection to Ireland. These same schools will ignore other holidays and events that are more salient to black children, such as Kwanzaa, deeming them "too ethnic."

Provide a broad listening repertoire to black boys that includes jazz, reggae, rhythm and blues, gospel, funk, symphonic works by black composers, rap, and soul. Chuck Jackson, a

1960s R & B singer, once told me that music in the black community "turns over" about once every eight years. Rap has been around for over twenty. Young people today admittedly say that they listen to rap more than R & B. Jazz and blues artists are often relegated to being "old school" and "too adult." Black parents, educators, and children should encourage *one another* to understand and appreciate the variety of music produced by black artists. Parents can encourage "listening nights" instead of "viewing nights" during which they share one another's favorite music.

Take opportunities to visit museums, library exhibits, and other community activities that present black history. When necessary, connect with Warrior Method parents to mount political influence that will force systems to provide such attractions. Art museums, libraries, and other cultural centers have large discretion over which exhibits they will mount and how long they will be displayed. Parents and teachers of black students should influence such decisions through performing volunteer activities and suggesting ideas for exhibits and displays.

Encourage black houses of worship to supplement your boys' education by having at least three hours of classes per week devoted to the study of black history. Most African-American faith communities celebrate the same holidays that schools do. They should go beyond that by offering Saturday morning classes that teach black history to young people. At an automobile plant not far from where I work, workers relocating from Japan opened Saturday schools for their children to ensure their continued understanding of Japanese culture while in Tennessee. Churches can be instrumental in teaching children black world history by offering similar courses.

On more than one occasion I have had the privilege of speaking in black churches during February, surrounded by white angels, Jesuses, and prophets. I point out to my audience the need to substitute these powerful images with black angels and religious figures in order to create a more balanced view of religion. Black faith communities can be extremely influential institutions in shaping the consciousness of black boys even before they go to school.

Provide educational films that teach the history of Africa, the period of enslavement, and its aftermath. The horrors of enslavement and the fate of its victims should be taught to black boys in a manner similar to what is taught to young Jewish children about the Holocaust. I know black parents who avoid exposing their sons to the horrors of enslavement, lynching, apartheid, and violence toward African Americans. This expensive proposition will be paid for by their development of a naive view of world history. Teaching this history should be done carefully, but it should be done. Black children who have an understanding of the "stony road" trod by their ancestors are better prepared to understand current challenges facing black communities around the world.

Expand images of Africa beyond those of famine, war, and disaster that characterize coverage of the continent by news organizations. Travelogues that include elephants, giraffes, and hyenas are good, but these limit the view of Africa as the proverbial "dark continent." Black children need to understand their connection to the continent by being exposed to its folklore, culture, customs, and people. They need to know their roots in West Africa so that they are rooted in their history. I am amused when I see European Americans who encourage their children to understand their Italian, French, German, or English roots yet belittle educators who do the same with black children's connection to Africa. Such attitudes develop the deeply held notion that Africa contributed virtually nothing to world history or culture. Fallacies such as these need to be corrected so that a healthy view of Africa can be instilled in the minds of black *and* white children.

I recently subscribed to a service from my cellular phone provider that automatically sends customized news about Africa directly to my phone. All of the short headlines were about war, famine, disease, and death. No human-interest stories. Nothing good. No uplifting stories about a continent whose beauty, people, and culture are some of the most diverse in the world. Those who glean the wire services looking for some good news about Africa would think that it is indeed the "dark continent" that has been imprinted on the minds of the world for the past five hundred years.

Encourage the wearing of African clothing at young ages. All parents complain about how their children dress. It is a part of growing up. The popularity of *Kente* cloth and other African fabrics makes it easier for parents to teach their sons about African clothing and its meanings. While dress is no indicator of cultural commitment, it can be an easy way to teach lessons about one's heritage. Green ties on St. Patrick's Day; red, white, and blue on the Fourth of July; and clothing decorated with Confederate flags are cultural statements about one's heritage. Clothing is an easy way to teach people about their history, and this includes black boys as well.

At a Black History Month speaking engagement I spoke to an

attractive black family who had agreed that on Fridays they would all wear African clothing to work or school. The parents as well as their two teenage sons saw the clothing as both a statement and a way of teaching the importance of connections to Africa. The father told me how they knew the meaning of the clothing, where it was from, and under which circumstances it was worn. Too often generalizations are made about the continent of Africa, rather than citing information pertaining to individual African nations. Ghanaian clothing, for example, differs from South African clothing, and both differ from that which is worn in East Africa.

The need for "raising black consciousness" among black children is not new and will remain as long as racism surrounds them. Consciousness building is a lifelong process that begins in early childhood. It is a subtle process that can occur under a variety of circumstances. Sitting at the dinner table, wandering through the grocery store, paying a bill, or watching television with black boys—all can be the backdrop for lessons on who they are, where they have been, and where they are going.

Finally, black boys should also be encouraged to talk about their feelings, both good and bad. This is particularly critical when it comes to their feelings about girls and women.

While more will be said about this later, young black boys must understand the importance of seeing females as part of the sacred male-female bond so common in precolonial Africa and so absent today. Writer and critic Ayi Kwel Armah talks about the beauty of the relationship between black men and women and argues in *Two Thousand Seasons* that the destroyers (white supremacists) were and are always attempting to disrupt the healthy development of black men and women with each other.

"There is no beauty but in relationships. Nothing cut off by itself is beautiful. Never can things in destructive relationships be beautiful.

All beauty is in the creative purpose of our relationships. All ugliness is in the destructive aims of the destroyer's arrangements."

Commitment

The effort of raising consciousness in black boys and in oneself will inevitably lead to a commitment to them. The idea that black boys are a "throwaway generation" and are expendable is often an unconscious reality in schools and institutions that deal with them. I once asked a workshop composed primarily of white elementary school teachers to write on slips of paper something they *did not* like to do as teachers, but not to include their names. When I read them aloud to the group, I saw on one, "I do not like to touch my black boys." I had to withhold my anger in front of the group as I read the statement, and I thought how unfortunate the black boys were in the class of this "teacher" who did not like to tie their unlaced shoe, or comfort them if they scraped their knee in a playground fall. Such feelings of loathing indicate the success of dehumanizing young black males even among elementary school teachers.

It is important to understand how criminalizing black males in America has a long and sordid history and reinforces negative stereotypes about them. Charshee McIntyre said that studying the imprisonment patterns of black males is a strong indicator of how representing black males as dangerous became a self-fulfilling prophecy. For example, although Africans in Pennsylvania made up only 2.4 percent of the population in 1800, the decennial censuses in Chart I indicate their population in the

CHART 1: PERCENTAGE OF BLACK MALES IN WALNUT STREET JAIL, 1790–1830

Year	% African American Male
1790	4.6%
1800	8.5%
1810	9.4%
1820	8.8%
1830	8.3%

Walnut Street Jail, known historically as "the cradle of modern penitentiaries."

Essentially, black males were "overrepresented" in the prison system two hundred years ago, the same way they are over-represented today. There is roughly a 4:1 historical ratio of black males in the general population to those in prison. This is a remarkably consistent pattern that has held steadily since such records have been kept. McIntyre notes how anyone who is committed to understanding contemporary black males must connect the dots between such esoteric data and the systems in place that create such patterns of incarceration. I agree. It is not a waste of time for the committed educator, parent, or social worker to read *what happened* to black men in this country in order to understand *what is happening* to black boys today.

A case in point: I got a call from a mother whose eleven-year-old son was expelled from school for "stealing $37.00 out of his teacher's purse." She had exhausted all of her appeals to get the suspension expunged from Todd's fifth-grade record. Todd was depressed when I saw him. An honor student with no blemishes on his record and no discipline problems, he simply happened to be the last student in the class on the day when his teacher's purse had been rifled. Added to the "incriminating" evidence was the fact that he had $50 on him at the time he was confronted about the missing money. Even though his mother had given him the $50 to pay a bill after school that day, her alibi was ignored, and a police officer dutifully took a "victim's report" from the white woman who reported the theft. Todd made perfect fodder for a system that is set on criminalizing black boys at the youngest age possible.

I had seen too many incidents like this before, and knew that many others had escaped my attention. There is one common element in how such scenarios are brought to the attention of therapists and attorneys, and that is if the child has a Warrior Method parent, teacher, or guardian. Todd's mother fit the description of such a parent. Single, poor, and living in public housing, she was obsessively involved with the education of her two sons. She called my office for an appointment. When she arrived, she had the necessary documents in the case and explained that she needed an advocate for her son so that this incident would not be on his record. Organized and angry, she told me that she believed that her son was innocent and that the teacher felt threatened by his assertive and intelligent behavior, particularly when it came to discussing racial issues in his social studies class.

They came to me on the first day of his suspension, and I was impressed with the confidence exhibited by both Todd and his mother. He didn't strike me as a thief; based solely on the evidence that they presented, I called the teacher, principal, and "downtown" for appointments to have his case reopened.

I have learned that systems, particularly educational systems, are often remarkably sloppy when they go after young black males. It is as if those who mistreat black boys feel sanctioned to do nearly anything to them with impunity. Todd was no exception. Poor record keeping, a weak black principal who was thankful for having a job at a predominantly white school, and a tired bureaucrat at administrative headquarters who simply wanted Todd, his mother, and me to go away were quick to have the charges expunged. The teacher wanted both her money and a criminal, and Todd happened to be handy. One week after the apology and a sanitized record, a *white* boy "turned himself in" after his mother discovered an amount of money larger than his allowance in his bedroom. *He* had been the last one in the teacher's classroom, not Todd, but somehow he received only a *reprimand* because he was "honest" in returning the money. It is impossible not to see a double standard at work in this case and in most cases involving how black and white boys are treated by educational and legal systems.

The second of the Four Cs—commitment—is achieved simply by doing the "right thing" with regard to black boys. Black boys are often without advocates in a nation frequently bent on demoralizing and destroying them physically, spiritually, and emotionally. For every Todd who is proven innocent, there are many other black boys who are falsely accused by persons who simply want them out of the way or because they fit a certain description. Commitment is putting the first C—consciousness—into action, and being unrelenting in the pursuit of justice for black boys. It emphasizes the heart rather than the head; knowledge of your son's character arises from the familiarity gained after being conscious of your son and the systems through which he must travel. There is only one indication of commitment to black boys: the willingness to intervene on their behalf at any level to enhance their life chances.

Cooperation

Cooperation in raising black boys takes place at several levels. Ideally it should involve several members of the immediate family—something that is diminishing as single parenting and divorce rates increase within African-American communities. Cooperation includes understanding the historical relationship that school systems played in educating black children, and how relationships between black men and black women were damaged by enslavement and its impact on the black family. The closeness necessary between outside agencies—most notably schools—and those raising black children is not understood as well as it should be. Those committed to raising Cinque's sons require a thorough understanding of how cooperative relationships both outside *and* inside black families are under assault by American institutions.

Cooperation and Black Schools

The African proverb "It takes a village to raise a child" is part of the national lexicon on how to raise at-risk children. From the White House to the street, the proverb is quoted to acknowledge how systems *and* parents are responsible for rearing children in America. Educator Jawanza Kunjufu cynically says that the proverb presupposes that there is a *functional* village to raise the child, a detail that is all too often lacking.

The destruction of the "village" took place over the past century as black families migrated north during the 1920s and 1930s and reinvented various institutions to accommodate their sense of community. The "storefront church" on the south side was the reincarnation of the one-room church in rural Mississippi. The country juke joint became the local honky-tonk as African Amer-

icans refined the blues and jazz born in the cotton fields of the
Deep South. Most regrettable during this transition was the
inability to duplicate educational systems that had been heavily
influenced by the presence of black colleges and universities such
as Hampton, Fisk, and Tougaloo. "Urban education" became
synonymous with black education and was associated with unresponsive administrations, inefficiency, and lack of materials.

The segregation patterns of the South persisted in the North,
however, and the ironic benefits of the entire *Plessy v. Ferguson*
era were that segregated systems actually allowed for a more
intact presentation of black culture and history to students. The
Lake Mohonk Conferences, June 4–6, 1890, and June 3–5, 1891,
give a clear understanding of the role of racism in the education
of black people. Held in upstate New York, they occurred
shortly after the period of enslavement to discuss the "Negro
Question." Rutherford B. Hayes, credited with the "Compromise of 1877," which effectively disenfranchised southern blacks
of nearly all of the gains of Reconstruction, convened the conferences and called for an emphasis on industrial education to
"uplift the Negro." What was important about these conferences
is that they saw African Americans as newly freed beasts of burden in need of guidance in how to be "good citizens." Part of the
historic Du Bois/Washington debate was Du Bois's disagree-
ment with the emphasis on industrial education at the expense
of the liberal arts. Du Bois and Woodson both saw education as
liberation and challenged the educational philosophy of Mohonk
that relegated African Americans to the subservience of a strictly
labor class.

"Lift Every Voice and Sing," part of the music repertoire of
most black children prior to *Brown,* was slowly phased out after
the decision. Likewise, black principals and other "role models"
were forced into early retirement due to the "merger" of black

and white schools during the 1960s and 1970s. In the South alone, some fifteen hundred black administrators lost their jobs directly because of these mergers, a fact often overlooked by integration advocates.

This should not be construed as a rationale for maintaining racially segregated school systems, but as an honest acknowledgment that *Brown v. Board* in 1954 forced African-American educators and parents to relinquish to faceless bureaucracies what control they did have over their children's education. Attempts to gain control over the damaging effects of the desegregation order took the form of demonstrations in the infamous 1968 Ocean Hill–Brownsville controversy in Brooklyn, New York. Warrior Method parents tried unsuccessfully to regain local control over curriculum development from a centralized bureaucracy that ignored the needs of the nearly all-black school district.

The cry for all-black schools, and, specifically, all-black male schools should be viewed as a historical correction over the problems associated with *Brown v. Board*. The "separate but equal" system that had existed for sixty years in the United States was "remedied" by moving bodies (black and white children) rather than bureaucracies. White schools were deemed superior to black schools and therefore "integrating" them with black children would assure higher learning and school performance. White schools with black children were thought to be the most efficient way of eliminating patterns of discrimination.

Predictably, the busing riots of the 1970s showed once again how deeply resistant many whites were to racially integrated education and exposed their underlying fears of miscegenation. What needed to be bused from white to black school districts were tax dollars that were unfairly distributed in ways that ensured the "inferiority" of black schools. *Time* magazine in a cover story timidly asked a few years ago if integration had "failed." The answer is yes, in that it did not address the educational needs of African-American children. Neither did it usher in the "Beloved Community" King called for in his historic "I Have a Dream" speech.

Cooperation Between Black Men and Women

Undoubtedly the greatest impact that racism had on Africans in the *Maafa* was the destruction of the African family, especially the relationship between men and women. The principle of "twoness" reflected in the literature and art of West African culture, where African-American ancestral ties lie, shows the sacredness of the relationship between men and women. On my visits to Ghana, I never fail to spend time watching men and women make *foo-foo*, a dumplinglike mixture of flour, oil, and yeast. The man plunges a six-foot pestle from above his head into the rounded bowl while the woman gracefully reshapes the dough with her nimble fingers. The rhythm of the process is hypnotic and illustrates the connection that must exist between a man and woman when making the bread. One seventy-five-year-old woman told me that never once had she seen a man or woman hurt while making the dumpling, though toes and fingers are at stake as the delicacy takes shape.

Similar balances exist among Ghanaian men and women who do a brisk trade in *Kente* cloth, a popular fabric among African Americans and symbolic of the ties between blacks in the United States and their ties with West Africa. Though viewed as "sexist" because only men are allowed to weave it, I have spoken to Ghanaian women and men who say that this division of labor is protective of the woman; the lower body is used in the making of the cloth and can strain the reproductive organs of women and lead to miscarriage if they are pregnant. The social balance is evidenced by the fact that women handle *all* the business associated with the cloth's packaging, distribution, and sales.

Black men and women in America can restore the historical balance between them by surrounding their sons with cultural artifacts and celebrations that reinforce a positive view of West Africa. They can encourage cooperative child rearing among themselves regardless of their marital status.

The "absent black father," though exaggerated in many instances by media, can continue an active role in his son's life, particularly as it relates to his education. Again it is important to mention that understanding how racism works to mutate relationships among blacks is critical in raising and educating healthy black boys in America.

Black boys will benefit from understanding the cooperative relationship between black men and women in the struggle against racism and the restoration of African values. There will be a diminished emphasis on material possessions such as "designer clothing" and athletic shoes that commodify black boys into becoming, as George Curry puts it, "advertising billboards for the clothing industry."

Cooperation should also focus on sharing parenting duties with single parents. In 1997, single women headed 47 percent of African American households, outnumbering married couples living together (46 percent) by 1 percent. The remaining 7 percent of households are headed by single men, thus making over half of black families (54 percent) single-parent households. This is the first time in American history that more African-American children are residing in homes with single parents than married couples.

It is also important to understand that parenting must be redefined to include a *functional* "village" for young black males. This village is the extended family that nurtured the black family during enslavement and beyond. Herbert Gutman has shown that, despite rumors to the contrary, the African American family remained remarkably intact during the years following enslavement. He argues that the idea of the disorganized black family discussed by Patrick Moynihan in 1965 was more myth than reality. What has occurred since the Vietnam War is an increase in single parenting, which coincides with the increased criminalization of African-American males and their subsequent incarceration.

This unbalanced black sex ratio (defined as the number of men per one hundred women) is at an all-time low (86:100) and does not include men who are gay, confirmed bachelors, with white women, or incarcerated. Rose Brewer, writing in the *Eighth Edition of the African American Almanac*, says:

> "The resulting ratio of approximately 86 males to every 100 females makes the matching of every African American female with a same-race male for the traditionally valued lifetime monogamous marriage a numerical impossibility—there are simply not enough African American men alive. When one removes from consideration those males who are gay, the proportion of eligible African American men for African American women dwindles even more.
>
> Further, when one counts the number of African American males who are poorly educated and therefore educationally mismatched for marriage to their relatively more highly educated African American female counterparts, the pool of eligible men shrinks even smaller. High

African American male unemployment rates further compound the problem . . . incarcerated single African American men are unavailable as marriage partners and African American men in prison who are married are unavailable to be at home with their families and/or provide for them . . . there were 221,000 African American male prison inmates in 1996. . . ."

Brewer's numbers should not be construed to mean that women must have a man in order to be complete. She simply points out the lack of choices that African-American women have if they desire heterosexual marriage and a traditional nuclear family. Black boys shoulder a disproportionate amount of the frustration since more single women are parenting without adult males to serve as role models. Much has been written and discussed about how young black males may become the inadvertent victims of the frustration that their mothers feel toward the absent fathers. In one scene from John Singleton's *Boyz in the Hood*, a single mother turns to her pubescent son and says, rather matter-of-factly, "Your daddy ain't shit, your brother ain't shit, and you ain't gonna be shit." The son is clearly frustrated and angry at the words. Although the movie was fictional, I have witnessed many such scenes both in public and in private.

The need to incorporate many people, particularly black men, in the rearing of black boys should be done in both informal and formal ways. Informally, African-American families have always solicited the help of relatives and friends for baby-sitting, entertainment, and household chores. What has been missing are more formal ways that take advantage of our community institutions. Following are some ways we can build the infrastructure of the "village" Hillary Clinton so famously spoke of:

Establish more "Mother's Day/Evening Out" programs at African-American churches so that single parents can get relief from parenting. Many black houses of worship in the African-American community already provide free day/night care on particular days so that mothers and fathers can leave their young children and enjoy a day alone or a night out on the town with their friends. This encourages a strong connection between houses of worship and single black parents and gives black elders a chance to mentor young children.

Make volunteering with black boys for five hours a month an initiation rite for all members of black social organizations. While most black organizations have volunteer service incorporated into their charters, they should require that new initiates work with black boys for five hours per month for a stipulated period. This will foster an attitude within the new member that working with young black boys is a priority and an obligation. It will also aid in establishing emotional ties with the new members, which will hopefully extend beyond the initiation period.

Encourage adoption among black houses of worship. The One Church, One Child Program of Illinois boasts twenty-two hundred black churches that have adopted more than six thousand youngsters in their churches. The program recruits families within its membership who wish to adopt black children, then works with adoption agencies for placement. This program is a model for what needs to be a nationwide effort to place black boys who are traditionally the least likely to be adopted into stable homes.

Create reading groups sponsored by black male civic and religious groups that support black boys reading about

African-American culture and life. If civic and religious groups can sponsor sports teams for black boys, they can expand their programs to include reading clubs as well. A good venue for such places is the increasing number of black-owned book-stores. Establishing a regular reading club makes good business sense for the owner and provides a perfect atmosphere for black boys. Libraries, too, are good locations for such clubs; once again, creating reading groups is a low-cost investment for black churches wishing to increase reading skills among their young members.

Because of the dwindling number of two-parent households, cooperative child rearing has become a central concern in the black family. Although national organizations such as 100 Black Men, black fraternities, and other groups are becoming more active in the cooperative rearing of black boys, more can be done. This goal should be high on the agenda of any black organization that claims as its purpose the alleviation of problems within African-American communities.

Community

At the end of the day, community may be the most important of all the Four Cs since it advocates Black and Gray Way parents challenging the systems that too often hurt, maim, and destroy self-esteem and, thus, the healthy development of black boys. Warrior Method parents understand the necessity of creating alternative systems to provide for the healthy development of their sons.

Political and social pressure on systems through which black boys pass should be monitored on several levels to ensure that no black boy becomes a victim of racism. It is amazing how little contemporary African Americans know about the history of education in their communities. The popular media exalts the histories of Booker T. Washington and George Washington Carver, as they should, but neglect to discuss the works of Carter G. Woodson, John Henrik Clarke, and Mary Church Terrell, who taught the importance of Warrior Method activism. What is even more astonishing is how current educators, both black and nonblack, lack understanding of how local, state, and federal governments actively sought, in deliberate and systematic ways, the disenfranchisement of black education.

Warrior Method parents and teachers must strive to teach those around them about African-American educational history so that what seems to be "radical" is viewed in the context of the historical struggle to provide quality education for black children. The confrontations in Little Rock, Ocean Hill, Brownsville, the University of Mississippi, and the University of Alabama are in the best tradition of pushing toward educational opportunities for black children. The civil rights movement itself was fueled primarily by struggles to integrate school systems that had legally excluded blacks since *Plessy*. The violence that resulted from integrating the Universities of Mississippi and Alabama is part of a long tradition of white resistance to the education of black children; it continues today with discussions of vouchers and charter schools. Warrior Method parents understand that only in rare instances have white school systems been seriously committed to educating black children. This is a difficult idea to accept, especially by White Way parents, but the proof exists in the historical record.

But more needs to be done. Medical care, decent housing, political empowerment, and affordable day care should be moved to the top of the agendas of those who want the best for black boys. Several specific strategies can be taught and adopted by black institutions to ensure that this occurs:

Monitoring and attending school board meetings in school districts. The importance of black parents being politically involved with local school boards cannot be overemphasized. Often only crises, such as the closing of a cherished school, bring black parents to school board meetings, and the overall flow of school board decisions is lost. Churches and other black civic organizations should send to school board meetings designated monitors, who then disseminate board decisions to their constituents. The names and addresses of each board member should be printed in newsletters and bulletins, so that between meetings parents can lobby on critical issues that affect their children.

Using Title VI of the 1964 Civil Rights Act to ensure the equitable distribution of federal dollars for local projects. Henri Brooks, former chair of the Tennessee State Black Caucus, says that Title VI of the 1964 U.S. Civil Rights Act is the most neglected part of the 1960s civil rights legislation. Title VI specifically calls for the equitable, nondiscriminatory distribution of federal funds to local governments. Under this act, municipalities are obligated to ensure that all segments of the community are represented on the boards responsible for the distribution of funds to local businesses, arts organizations, social programs, etc. Organizations serving the needs of black people have overlooked their right to sue under this legislation. Tracing how federal funds were used at the state and local level could provide the basis for a class-action lawsuit that could result in more dollars for programs targeting black youth.

Creating political action committees (PACs) that serve the special interests of the black community. Political action in black communities has a long and rich history that should continue by increasing the number of PACs for targeted purposes. PACs have become a political reality in the United States and blacks can use them to influence the outcome of elections and legislation that affect their lives. Black elected officials should place a high priority on the formation of PACs, and these officials should educate their constituents about their need.

Both the 1996 and 2000 elections showed the importance of black persons engaging cooperatively in national elections. News organizations focused only tangentially on the disenfranchisement of black people during the 2000 presidential election, yet it was the biggest story of the political year. The denial of access to voting targeting black and Latino voters, especially in Florida, is illustrative of the fragility of America when it comes to ensuring the rights of persons of color. No less than the provisions of the Fifteenth Amendment were at stake, yet Americans—white and black—thought that "accepting the results" was more important than ensuring the rights of disenfranchised voters. Young Warriors should be thoroughly versed regarding the events in the United States during November and December of 2000. They should understand how there is no end to the lengths to which white supremacists will go in order to limit the voices of blacks, even though it may mean scuttling the law and ignoring the Constitution. Some attribute the major congressional shift of 1996, particularly in the House of Representatives, to the large turnout of black voters. Similarly, more accountability from Democratic candidates should be demanded by black voters since an overwhelming number (90 percent) support the party. Black elected officials—overwhelmingly Democratic—need to get voters registered and educate their supporters. In addition, they must agitate for national Democratic leaders to devote more attention to the needs of black communities at all times.

Targeting for selective buying businesses that have a history of harassing and/or underemploying African Americans, particularly boys. The boycott remains a most effective way to achieve equity for African Americans. Nike, South Carolina, NBC, and other entities have yielded to requests for representation on boards and television shows, and have agreed to the removal of offensive symbols, all due to boycotts. Nothing affects quicker change than a focused effort by African Americans practicing selective buying of a company's product. Clothing companies whose markets are urban black males are particularly vulnerable to selective buying campaigns, and they should be made aware of the ramifications of their practices toward our youth and our collective power.

Systematically writing congressional representatives to make sure they are responsive to legislation that affects the lives of black children. One of the most effective yet neglected political-action strategies is as old as America: writing letters to lawmakers. The Internet and fax machines make this even easier, and groups such as the National Black Child Development Institute (www.nbcdi.org) actually monitor at the national level legislation that will have impact on black youth.

Mailing lists of key political figures must contain the names and addresses of Warrior Method parents. The nonglamorous work of parsing the esoteric language of bills and legislative agendas is time-consuming and tedious, but it has to be done. I have participated in and encouraged others in letter-writing campaigns that were highly successful in blocking legislation that was egregious to young African-American males.

Creating booster clubs that encourage the purchase of computer technology for black children. The recently discussed "digital gap" between whites and people of color is primarily economic. It is important that African-American children become acquainted at young ages with what arguably will be the most important educational and cultural revolution in the first quarter of the twenty-first century. I hope that Bill Gates's contribution of $1 billion to close this gap will motivate others to do likewise. Gifts of computers or laptops instead of VCRs and game machines are a good investment in our boys' future. Competitions sponsored by black civic organizations should have computers as first, second, and third prizes. Historically black colleges and universities, often located in depressed economic areas, can build educational bridges between their computer labs and the community. The goal of all these efforts is to keep African-American children at a pace that will make them technologically competitive with other ethnic groups.

Organizing groups of African-American houses of worship to build educational facilities to meet the needs of black children. I recently spoke to a group of black ministers who asked what they could do as a group to help black boys in their community. I told them to place 50 percent of their fourth Sunday offering into an escrow account for one year, and with this initial capital, build a K-12 school. I then told them to continue the offering indefinitely to pay for the salaries of the teachers and administrators who would be employed in the school. The look of surprise on their faces was followed by many reasons why this was too great of a project. One minister said this was a "larger idea than what they had in mind" and that they thought the creation of a sports team or some other small project would be more feasible. I estimated that within the room there was conservatively $500,000 per week being placed in banks by the churches. I was essentially asking them for half of that during one offering to go for a school that would educate our children. There was resistance to this suggestion because of the symbolic role that black church buildings play in African-American communities. They are often seen as monuments to a minister's business prowess and are rarely used more than two or three times per week.

This is not an indictment of misplaced priorities among black clergy but a call to rearrange existing priorities relative to educating black boys. Most black churches have some form of educational outreach ranging from day care to tutoring. In some cases churches run full-time accredited schools, paid for by members of the congregation. The advent of the "mega" black church—churches with more than three thousand members—should make building schools easier than in the past. Forming educational consortiums across denominations can bring smaller houses of worship into the educational process without burdening them financially.

Encouraging black houses of worship to create credit unions for the communities they serve. One of the principles of the African-American holiday *Kwanzaa* is *Ujamaa* (pronounced UU-jah-mah), and is translated "cooperative economics." Similar to the cooperative education of children that churches can establish, credit unions can be built that will help members regain a good credit rating, purchase homes, and establish small businesses. I know of several large urban churches who have done this without indulging in the dubious practice of creating "prosperity ministries" which often emphasize dollars over spiritual growth.

Placing money in African-American-owned banks. While many communities do not have black-owned banks, those that do should actively court black dollars of individuals, businesses, and churches. Individuals should also do as much business with these banks as possible so that community money can be reinvested in the community. This is a simple yet effective way of creating wealth for impoverished black communities, and it is similar to what other ethnic communities have done. Where black banks do not exist, community leaders should cultivate a close relationship between the institutions they represent and bank officers so that projects that are directly related to the surrounding community can be realized.

Sponsoring summer-abroad study programs in Africa. In my years as a college professor, I have been fortunate to see many of my students travel to Africa, a rewarding experience because it brings an abstract notion to life. I have witnessed firsthand the changes that take place in these students. They return energized and committed to teaching their peers more about the language, customs, and culture of Africa. I know black civic groups that sponsor winter tours to Europe for skiing vacations but avoid sending groups to Ghana, Senegal, or other West African nations. Most people—black and nonblack—after being fed *anti-African* ideas from the first day of their formal education, never consider Africa as a travel destination. Sponsoring tour groups with children and adults is an investment in their future; it gives them a much more realistic view of the ancestral home of African Americans.

Are these "big" agenda items? Yes. Are they feasible for all communities? No. Are there historical precedents for all of them? Yes. In the final analysis, community, the last of the Four Cs, encourages those interested in the well-being of black boys to become politically and socially involved in their lives. That's it.

The previous chapters outlined the necessary values, ideas, and knowledge to raise black boys. The following chapters, entitled the Seasons of Our Sons, will outline what our sons face as they grow from boys to men.

4

The Seasons of Our Sons: Spring, Conception to Four

Ole Missus and young Missus told the little slave children that the stork brought the white babies to their mothers, but that the slave children were all hatched out from buzzards' eggs. And we believed it was true.
—KATIE SUTTON, SLAVE[*]

Conception Through Four Years

The first rite of passage for humans is birth, and for black boys the first year of life is one of the most dangerous on earth. The outmoded term "third-world nation" is often used to describe countries in the so-called "developing world." These developing countries have high infant mortality rates. *The mortality rate for African-American baby boys during their first year of life is comparable to that of infants born in Asia, Africa, and South America.* As with other statistics, if the infant mortality rate for white male babies were identical to that of black male babies, there is no doubt in my mind that a national crisis would be declared and millions of dollars would be spent on pre- and postnatal care to ensure that white male babies would survive their first year of

[*]Recorded during the Federal Writers' Project of the 1930s and 1940s. Referenced in James Mellon's *Bullwhip Days* (1988), Avon Books.

life. Chart 2 illustrates the comparative statistics for black and white male infancy mortality rates in the United States; Chart 3 gives data on how black infant mortality rates compare with other countries. The most alarming statistic is that the gap between black and white male infants actually *increased* during the period from 1980 through 1996. In other words, by the late 1990s black male babies were actually dying faster than their white counterparts during their first year of life than those babies born at the beginning of the Reagan administration. If the current trend continues, by 2050 black male infants will be dying three times faster during their first year of life than white males.

The consequences of mortality rates ultimately translate into significantly lower life expectancy for African-American males. Currently, the worst place to live in the United States if you are a black male is Washington, D.C., where my brothers live an average of only 57.53 years. By comparison, only seven of the

CHART 2: BLACK AND WHITE MALE INFANT MORTALITY RATES IN THE UNITED STATES, 1980–1996

Year	Black Males	White Males	% Higher BM/WM
1980	24.2	12.1	200%
1982	22.5	11.1	202%
1984	20.7	10.4	199%
1986	20.9	9.9	211%
1988	20.0	9.4	212%
1990	19.6	8.5	230%
1992	18.4	7.7	238%
1994	17.5	7.2	243%
1996	16.0	6.7	238%

Source: *National Vital Statistics Report,* Vol. 47, No. 9, November 10, 1998 most populous nations on earth have lower life expectancy rates: Bangladesh (53.5 years), Ethiopia (51.5 years), Myanmar (Burma) (54.5 years), Pakistan (56.5 years), Sudan (53.0 years), Tanzania (52.5 years), and Zaire (54.0 years). India, with an average life expectancy of 57.0 years, compares favorably to the life expectancy of black males living in Washington, D.C.

But it gets worse. Even though the average life expectancy for Americans is 75.37, with male life expectancy at 71.83, there is no state in the country where the average black male can expect to live beyond the age of 70. The state that enjoys the highest rate for black men is Colorado (68.96 years), with Massachusetts following close behind with 68.17 years. Outside of the District of Columbia, Pennsylvania has the lowest life expectancy rate for black men, at 63.33 years. My father succeeded in matching the national average of life expectancy by dying at the age of sixty-four, and as I write this, I know that if I

CHART 3: SELECTED INFANT MORTALITY RATES FOR VARIOUS COUNTRIES

Country	Infant Mortality Rate
Japan	6
Sweden	6.4
Switzerland	7.5
France	8.2
Singapore	8.8
United States (WHITE)	9.4
Italy	11.4
Greece	14.1
Cuba	15.0
United States (BLACK)	18.4

Source: World Health Organization

live beyond thirteen more years, I will flirt with death nearly every day. That I had my first heart attack at fifty years of age raised few eyebrows among my African-American friends and colleagues. My life expectancy, and that of all black males, is shorter than everyone else's.

While these statistics are sobering, they also engender anger among black men and women. Black children simply have no business dying twice as fast as white children, and black male infant mortality rates should be going down, not up. At the most superficial level, these data reflect the persistence of racism in one of the two most fundamental life journeys that all of us make—birth (the other being death), and indicate the low value that America places on black males.

Turning again to Washington, D.C., the black male's life expectancy is comparable to that of the entire U.S. population in 1920. This eighty-year lag in my brothers' life expectancy compared to the rest of the nation will worsen during the present century. If current trends continue, by 2100, while the average life expectancy for all Americans will approach one hundred years, black men will live only about as long as contemporary Americans—seventy-five years.

CHART 4: MALFORMATIONS BY RACE PER 10,000 BIRTHS

Malformation	Blacks	Whites
Anencephaly	2.1	3.0
Spina bifida without anencephaly	3.3	5.1
Cleft palate without cleft lip	3.7	5.9
Cleft lip without cleft palate	4.4	9.7
Clubfoot	19.9	27.5
Down's syndrome	6.5	8.5

Source: *Health Status of Minorities and Low-Income Groups,* Third Edition, p. 106.

One could view these appalling data as support for the notion that black boys suffer from genetic inferiority. While such a racist notion lacks support, it is interesting to note rarely cited data comparing birth defects among African-American children with those of their white counterparts. The infrequency of such studies could be construed as a fear of white neonatologists and other health researchers to discuss how genetic factors and race interact in the biological development of black and white children. Blacks are consistently lower than whites in nearly all categories of birth defects. Chart 4 illustrates selected malformations at birth by race. These statistics illustrate that black male infants are not dying because of genetic anomalies but because of environmental stressors—all of which are preventable. The conspiratorial silence on comparative birth defects among boys is related to the health care industry having to point a finger at itself for its negligence in providing adequate health care for black males.

Black Boys at Birth

Though starting life with a less-than-average chance of surviving the first year, black male babies can be protected even before birth to make their first life passage easier. With the first announcement of pregnancy, mothers should establish a group or a Birthing Circle that will provide the support and care to ensure a trouble-free pregnancy and birth. If the mother-to-be is married, her husband should be included in the circle. If single, the mother should look to both male and female relatives and friends for the community birthing. To some degree, this already occurs in families *informally.* I suggest a far more formalized structure that would include specific assignments to members of the circle. These circles should have between seven and ten persons and should be balanced with both men and women. Assignments within the Birthing Circle should include everything from pre- to postnatal care and support to home care for the expectant mother. The structure of the circle should involve the following:

Designating a person to monitor the mother's prenatal care, i.e., making sure that appointments are kept and accompanying her on doctor visits during the pregnancy. As previously stated, the infant mortality rate for black boys is preventable if proper prenatal care becomes a habit starting at conception. The Birthing Circle ensures that, at conception, a village is created that will guarantee that the mother has a strong support system for her child. Assigning a relative or an elder to accompany the expectant mother to her ob/gyn helps to foster good medical habits in the mother.

Designating a person (male or female) to join the mother for prenatal Lamaze, nutrition, or exercise classes. Much has been written about the "naturalness" of birth, even though physicians view it as a medical procedure. A circle member can explore with the mother the widely used Lamaze Method, other holistic techniques such as Leboyer's birth without violence system, and midwifery while simultaneously educating her about the birthing process. A mother-to-be needs to follow a balanced diet throughout her pregnancy, and a circle member should assist with her nutrition education if necessary. Circle members should discourage the use of harmful products such as liquor and tobacco. Finally, the mother-to-be should keep a "diet diary" whenever possible, so that her closest friend or relative can make sure that she is receiving the nutrition both she and her baby need.

Designating a person to serve as a backup for completing the paperwork associated with childbirth. This includes health insurance, medical records, and paperwork required by either a midwife or hospital. The blizzard of paperwork associated with pre- and postnatal care, as well as birth itself, should not be a frustration for the mother. A circle member should assist so that unexpected expenses, insurance inquiries, and bills do not occupy a lot of her time.

Designating a person to serve as an information specialist on such things as naming, postbirth ceremonies, and health information. This should be a person acquainted with rites-of-passage ceremonies and African-centered naming ceremonies. Since Birthing Circles by design are African-centered, many persons can participate in this. The traditional "baby shower" can be supplemented with discussions about names, birth ceremonies, and spiritual matters associated with birth.

Designating a person to accompany the mother into the delivery room. This last point is very critical. The most obvious person to attend the birth of the child is the father, but often this is not an option. In that case, a family member or a close male friend should be with the mother at the time of delivery. None of these suggestions presuppose the "helplessness" of the black mother, nor do Birthing Circles have anything to do with Western notions of "sexism." They are, rather, the earliest expression of the male/female participation in the child's life and should accompany the baby from the day of conception.

Before delivery, friends and/relatives should throw an African-centered baby shower. Books, clothing, music, and other items may be added to the traditional gifts of diapers, formula, and other baby supplies. Members of the Birthing Circle should attend this gathering, and visit at the time of delivery.

Naming Our Children

The increased popularity of giving black children African names is a positive sign of our increasing consciousness of our African pasts. My own children—Omari Lateef, Sharifa Hasin, and Faraji Khalid—all have names meaningful to them that my wife and I chose carefully to reflect our hopes and aspirations for their lives. The name of my oldest son, Omari Lateef, means "high and gentle." His mother and I wanted him to be successful and fair in what he does. He is now a practicing attorney. The name Sharifa Hasin, my only daughter, means "nobly beautiful," and recognizes that we wanted her to be strong and charismatic in the work she does. She is in dental school. The name of my youngest son, Faraji Khalid, means "he will bring us peace," and while he and I have doubted that at times, his mother and I felt he came at a time of great stress in our lives, so his name reflects our hopes. He is in college now, with hopes of becoming a recording engineer. West African naming ceremonies are important and sacred; the naming of a child is a major event among various clans and groups.

We must name our children with the utmost care and in a calm and meditative fashion. Too often, parents name children *phonetically*, rather than *culturally*, which results in meaningless names and bizarre spellings. Comedians can joke about many of these names because the naming has been done in the White Way. "Judahrusalem," "Lamonakeesha," and "Baramalooma," though phonetically pleasing, supply little information to the black child as to who he or she is. While it is not automatic that a child named Rolaqueesha will grow up confused about her racial identity, the most basic indicator given to a child, other than gender, should not be done in a haphazard or uninformed way.

Early Hurdles for Black Boys

The first two years of a black boy's life are fraught with dangers. After birth, black boys frequently lack adequate health care. Chart 5 indicates the persistence of mortality beyond birth among black male children. We will find that there is only one age range during which black males outlive their white counterparts—eighty-five years and older. Why black octogenarians live longer than their white peers is still unknown, but research could give valuable insight into this anomaly.

The Birthing Circle should continue through the newborn's first year of life. Members should encourage the mother to make sure that all scheduled immunizations take place; this is another area where black males fall short. The Birthing Circle should also encourage the mother to exercise and regain her prepregnancy

---

CHART 5: NUMBER OF INFANT, NEONATAL, AND POST NEONATAL MORTALITY RATES IN MALES, 1996

(Rates are [infant <1 year], [neonatal <28 days], [postnatal 28 days to 11 months] per 100,000)

	Infant	Neonatal	Post neonatal
Black Males	1,604.5	1,044.9	559.6
White Males	666.6	430.8	235.7

Source: *National Vital Statistics Report*, V. 47, No. 9, November 1998 figure; many black women report that after their pregnancy it is difficult to care for their newborn child and adhere to a diet and exercise routine.

Everyone in the Birthing Circle should read to the infant during the first year of his life. Music should also play an important role in the young child's development. Exposure to stimulating music, such as soft jazz and West African pieces, can attune his young mind to appreciate a variety of music in later years. New research also shows that infant massage and other forms of touch play a major role in the development and socialization of children. While infant massage is still quite common among West African cultures, it has all but disappeared among Africans in America. Black boys, in particular, need to be touched and held so that they develop a sense of openness in their relationships with others, particularly girls and women.

The spring of a young black male's life can be best described as stormy. But the dangers can be minimized if simple precautionary and preventative steps are taken. We will see in the following chapters how the remaining seasons of our sons' lives also contain dangers that can be prevented. Joseph Cinque was faced with similar odds when he was kidnapped from his homeland during the spring of 1839. He faced dangers while in the hull of the ship, during his captivity, and even as he journeyed back to his home in Sierra Leone. His children can overcome similar dangers if they are surrounded by parents, teachers, friends, and relatives who truly care about their well-being.

5

The Seasons of Our Sons: Summer, Ages 5–12

> *No one sends a child on a difficult errand and gets angry if he does not perform it well.*
>
> —ASHANTI PROVERB

Ages 5–12: Chad

I was in the middle of my psychology internship at the notorious Robert Taylor Homes on Chicago's Southside. They were indeed "projects" since they seemed an "experimental" way of imprisoning their occupants in gloomy twenty-story buildings, with depressing fenced-in breezeways that prevented accidental or intentional falls to the debris-laden concrete sidewalks below. I chose the internship because I had been raised in a similar neighborhood, and I felt that my experiences growing up on the east side of Cleveland would benefit the children I was to see.

The decrepit elevators, reeking of urine, were dangerous places to be, and most of the residents avoided them when possible. Only the foolish rode them alone. The Head Start children to whom I was assigned were all housed on the first floor, which was clean and very well kept by a staff dedicated to the children in their care. I saw children in their classroom and in their homes. Most of the knowledge I had gained in my clinical psychology classes at the University of Chicago was better left at the doors of the apartments; almost none of it had any relevance to either the children or the adults there.

I saw whoever wanted to see me, despite the injunction of my professor to "focus" on the children in the Head Start program. I ignored his advice because there was a desperate need for mental health services in many of the tenants. I knew I was violating the strict rules of my future profession by counseling the residents, but I also knew that no one at Robert Taylor Homes cared about this. I supplied what counseling I could with the limited resources at my disposal. I continued in this way for several months; I helped parents develop study habits in their children, men to get jobs, boys to get their first jobs, and adolescents to cultivate an interest in museums and other educational facilities.

Rumor spread quickly that a "cool" psychologist was seeing children there, and over the course of the semester-long internship, I saw children, adolescents, and adults suffering from the posttraumatic stresses of living in the dangerous, overcrowded conditions of the homes. It was apt that the horror film *Candyman* would later be set in Cabrini-Green, not far from these homes; monsters haunted these breezeways and elevators in the form of drug addiction, alcoholism, abuse, and homicide.

One day, the teachers and I decided to take the children for a long walk down State Street, something that many of the children did not get to do on a regular basis. As we were exiting the cavernous quadrangle of buildings, we saw a strange sight on the vandalized playground about fifty yards from the Head Start office. There, on the nearly broken-down swing set, was a beautiful young mother laughing wildly and swinging so hard that she was nearly parallel to the bars high above her head. The pathological environment she was in contrasted with her stunningly beautiful twenty-something face, which seemed strangely twisted above her threadbare winter coat. What captured our attention, however, was the little boy who was screaming and clinging desperately to her coat in fear of being flung out of her lap and onto the pavement.

Swinging up and down, she seemed to be carrying on a conversation with unseen people. I ran over to the swing, trying to figure out how I could get them both down without harm. I was afraid to grab the swing from behind, worried that its momentum would throw the little boy away from his mother. Instead, I went to the front of the swing and asked the mother to slow down or her child would fall. She looked at me, laughed, said "No!" then propelled the swing even higher. Her uncontrolled laughter, disheveled look, and conversation with voices no one else could hear made it obvious that she was an reinstitutionalized mental patient, who had fallen through the ever-widening human service cracks.

I asked her why was she swinging so high with her son, and she said that she "had to teach him early that the world was a hard place to live in and that he had to be hard in order to survive." I asked her what her son's name was, and she screamed "Chad!" Then she yelled at him to hold on real tight. For a split second I thought about the evils of a world that taught such harsh lessons so early in life. I yelled out to her that there were other ways to teach such lessons; my fellow teachers hollered that she could kill her child if she didn't come down immediately. Enjoying the attention, she swung even higher toward the sky and she laughed aloud at us. I told my companions to surround the swing in order to maximize our chances of catching the hysterical little boy in case he fell.

I stationed myself in front of the swing, ready to catch it as it soared above my head. Suddenly the young mother screamed, "That's enough for today!" and began to bring her maniacal swinging to a halt. As quickly as was safe, I grabbed her terrified son, who now held me even tighter than he had his mother. The women with me immediately got on her case, and the children from the Head Start class watched the entire episode. They asked her if she was crazy; the woman nodded assent and assured them that she was. Stepping in, I asked her why she felt it necessary to put her son's life in danger. I asked her if she had meant what she said while she was up in the air, and she said she had. She calmly replied that no one but *she* could teach her son how bad the world was, and that, had she been swung like that when she was small, she wouldn't have "wound up in a mental institution." This young mother thought that her son's experience on the swing would teach him that feeling good could often wind up making him feel bad.

This is what had happened to her. She then *asked* me if she could hold her son, and while I had no right to keep him from her, I hesitated until Chad turned from me and opened his arms to his mother. I gently handed him to her and watched as she hugged him closely. They both started laughing and crying. I told her to stop by the Head Start office and visit me. She nodded, but I knew that I would never see her or her son again.

That incident haunted me for years. I cannot walk past a playground without being reminded of that cool spring day. What has truly haunted and saddened me is that she was right. "America wasn't gonna give Chad any breaks in anything." Since that day I have witnessed often just how right she was.

Massaging the Numbers

The polished and sophisticated statistics of the performance of black boys in elementary and middle school ignores the violence that confines them to a statistical netherworld inhabited by uncaring teachers, bloated bureaucracies, and violent upbringings. African-American boys have been endangered since they were first stolen from the shores of Africa nearly five centuries ago. In *Origin of Species by Means of Natural Selection,* Charles Darwin said, "If the differences among human beings is not due to biology but to our institutions then great is our sin." In other words, either black boys are *genetically* predisposed to commit crimes, sell drugs, and become fathers early on, or there is something seriously wrong with the institutions through which they move from birth to adulthood.

One of the most remarkable surprises about black boys is that their academic performance through the first four years of school is fairly good. Since 1969, the National Assessment of Educational Performance (NAEP), commonly referred to as the "nation's report card," has been the standard by which educational achievement by race and gender is measured. Though large gaps exist among the various students measured at fourth-, eighth-, and twelfth-grade levels, the 1998 scores of black students are very different from those of 1994. It is encouraging to note that at grade four, the only significant increase among racial and ethnic groups is observed for black students whose average reading score in 1998 was higher than in 1994. Another weakness of the NAEP is that statistics are kept on several variables, but they are not broken down by race *and* gender. Chart 6 shows NAEP writing scores by grade and ethnicity. Only inferences can be drawn from this national report card on the academic achievement of black males, since such statistics are not delineated in the database. What is more interesting, however, is research on why achievement levels for black boys are so low.

Jason Osborne's 1997 study comparing black, white, and Latino achievement found that black boys experience an "emotional withdrawal" from academics at a greater rate than do whites or Latinos. Black boys exhibiting intellectual prowess are often teased by peers, due to a cultural emphasis on macho behavior. An environment that does not encourage intellectual growth often supports boys' emotional disengagement from school. Parents not participating in school meetings, peers who have weak academic goals, and uncaring teachers are ingredients in the educational crucible that obviates effective learning. A curious finding in the study, however, is that even though the grades of these boys plummeted, the psychological protocols used to measure their self-esteem remained the same over the four years and in some cases actually increased. Claude Steele, a black psychologist at Stanford, found similar results. He points out that powerful stereotypes over "being smart" in the African-American community trigger anxiety and academic withdrawal on the part of black youngsters, particularly young black males in late elementary and middle school. Over the years I have seen many black boys in these grades ridiculed and deemed "less masculine" for earning good grades. These boys often struggle between making good grades and being accepted by friends who see good grades as "acting white." "Let's get stupid" is more than a phrase uttered on the dance floor. Jawanza Kunjufu and other educators have written about the false macho, encouraged by black boys' peers at ever decreasing ages, which rewards brawn and discourages brains.

Even though Herculean efforts have been made during the

Chart 6: NAEP Writing Scores by Race and Grade, 1998   Scale = 0–300

Ethnic Group	Grade 4
White	157
Black	131
Latino	134
Asian/Pacific Islander	164
American Indian	138

	Grade 8
White	158
Black	131
Latino	131
Asian/Pacific Islander	159
American Indian	132

	Grade 12
White	156
Black	134
Latino	135
Asian/Pacific Islander	152
American Indian	129

past ten years on presenting the realities of paid athletic competition as an opportunity for African-American boys, there are powerful incentives that dissuade them from believing these odds. Academic achievement falls even lower in the ranks when you add hip-hop culture's powerful influence, which often but not always encourages black macho behavior at the expense of academic achievement. It is ironic that since 1981, when Grandmaster Flash and the Furious Five's powerful lyrics in "The Message" described an urban world in which there was resistance to the temptation of "going under," much of rap has abandoned its political roots and become highly commercialized. Public Enemy, Dead Prez, and Goodie Mobb are notable exceptions to this, but the signifying that took place during the mid-1990s represented in the deaths of Tupac Shakur and Biggie Smalls had a lasting impact on the image of hip-hop. Parents should listen to rap while they encourage their children to listen to artists who still bring a powerful message of political awareness and African-centered consciousness to their music.

I believe that the sharp decline in African-American boys' academic achievement is due to factors associated with their transition into puberty. Along with peer pressure to perform athletically, there is a disturbing yet rarely discussed issue at work in the disregard for and stigma attached to a black boy who excels academically.

The late black psychologist Charles Thomas was the first to discuss how the sexual development of young black males threatens their mostly white and female teachers. Thomas argued that the societal taboo against black male/white female sexuality creates apprehension in white females, to the point that they fear its emergence in the black boys they teach.

Keep in mind that the primary instructors of black elementary and middle school boys are white females; the dynamics of this relationship are rarely investigated in trying to understand the decline in standardized test scores among pubescent black males. On more than one occasion, I have heard white female teachers refer to ten- to twelve-year-old black boys as "lady killers," "sexy," and "drop-dead gorgeous"—labels that go far beyond boosting self-esteem. On one occasion, after I conducted a workshop with teachers from a southern metropolitan area, a young white instructor approached me and said that she had a "crush" on one of her students. She looked to be in her mid-twenties, and I asked her what grade she taught. Meekly, she said, "Fifth." I asked her who the boy was, and she said that he was an eleven-year-old black boy. I was both shocked and angry and asked her how this was influencing her work with him. She told me that she tried to "avoid" him as much as possible, and that she was doing her best to "stay out of his way." I asked her if she thought her behavior and attitude were hurting him academically. She said they were, and that was why she was seeking advice. I told her that that she needed to examine herself to find out what motivated her feelings. She thanked me and walked away hurriedly, seemingly ashamed of what she had just told me.

Though anecdotal, I believe that unconscious sexuality is a neglected factor in understanding the dramatic decline of academic success. It should be added to the list of "explanatory factors" influencing black boys' academic performance, which has included genes, poverty, nutrition, parenting, and poor academic preparation.

While we have seen recent scandals involving older female teachers raping young boys, little has been done to measure this taboo subject across racial lines; the research would have to rely on self-reported data and would, of course, involve minors. I have spoken to other black educators about this subject, and many of them tell how they have overheard white female teachers talk in sexual terms about their black male students. The sexual anxiety felt by many of these teachers could easily translate into rejection and avoidance of their pubescent black male students. As stated earlier, the fascination with black sexuality has a long history in America; even though it is a difficult topic, its discussion would shed light on many issues.

Violence, Health, and Athletics

Separating violence from health issues is impossible when talking about young black boys. According to the 1996 study of the ten leading causes of death by the National Center for Injury Prevention and Control (NCIPC) in Atlanta, Georgia, in 1994, there were 416 homicides among youth ages ten to fourteen years and 8,116 homicides among youth ages fifteen to twenty-four. Black males were victims in 32 percent of all homicides among youth ages ten to fourteen and 52 percent of all homicides among youth ages fifteen to twenty-four. The 1995 Carnegie Council on Adolescent Development study, entitled Great Transitions: Preparing Adolescents for a New Century, found that the firearm homicide rate for ten- to fourteen-year-olds more than doubled between 1985 and 1992 (from 0.8 per 100,000 population to 1.9 per 100,000 population). For black males, the rate increased from 3.0 to 8.4 per 100,000 population during the same period, and from 1980 to 1992, the rate of suicide among young adolescents (ages ten to fourteen) increased 120 percent, with the most dramatic increases among black males (300 percent) and white females (233 percent).

In 1992, the Centers for Disease Control and Prevention (CDC) argued empirically that violence is a public health problem, and ignited a firestorm of response when it declared that handguns were directly connected to the high incidence of homicidal violence in the United States, particularly among young African-American males. The report viewed handguns,

like cigarettes, as a "health hazard" and was prophetic in predict-
ing that both industries would be sued because of the danger
they posed to Americans.

If it sounds like a litmus test, it is. Handguns are the primary
instrument of death for young black boys. The gun has become
romanticized among African-American communities in films
and music. This insidious blend of guns and media poses a
health hazard for black boys during the summer and fall years of
their lives (from ages five through eighteen). During these years,
the social pressures placed in black boys' paths begin to "show"
them how American society expects them to act. The lessons
taught are that violence, athleticism, and entertainment are their
primary choices in life. In this section I will discuss the importance of providing a counterbalance to the harmful and misleading images and messages from the all-powerful media. Media
educates children *and* socializes them, and part of this socialization involves how children perceive persons from different racial
and ethnic backgrounds. When adolescents watch television and
other visual media, they are strongly influenced by the racial and
gender stereotypes presented to them. Not much has changed
since Manuel Alvarado, Robin Gutch, and Tana Wollen found in
1987 that black characters on television are usually portrayed in
four different ways: exotic, dangerous, humorous, and pitiable.
Although African Americans appear more frequently on television than they once did, a 1990 study by George Gerbner and
Nancy Signorelli, of the Universities of Pennsylvania and
Delaware, found that they are often depicted negatively, as
criminals or victims of violent crimes. *Atlantic Monthly* has
dubbed Gerbner the "Man Who Counts the Killings," and his
Annenberg Center research is rigorous and well documented.
Known mostly for documenting how many murders children
watch by the time they are twelve, Gerbner has meticulously

coded the presence and images of all ethnic groups and both genders on television for years.

In 1999, the National Association for the Advancement of Colored People (NAACP) issued scathing indictments of the networks for the lack of people of color on their prime-time shows. The networks responded to this charge by introducing new characters and expanding the roles of black, Latino, and Asian actors in their evening shows. While the nation's leading civil rights organizations should sustain such political pressure, they should place additional emphasis on encouraging parents of black children to alter their viewing habits altogether; black children, particularly boys, watch far too much television. The expectation that adding a few ethnic characters to prime-time network television will reverse the damage already done by a medium that has been a primary shaper of negative ethnic images sounds like a compromise rather than a comprehensive solution. Raising Warriors must include implementing realistic strategies to educate black boys on how media manipulates their images. Teachers and parents can structure "no-TV nights" and replace them with individual and group activities that foster a positive self-image.

The most obvious instrument for doing this is the computer. The widening "technological gap" between blacks and whites can be partially narrowed if parents and community groups invest in computers for young African Americans. TV, VCRs, DVDs, and other high-tech pieces of equipment are often more integrated in the lives of our boys than are computers. The information highway is a wide boulevard through the African-American community and it is gratifying that the traffic increase has much to do with people of color. The active learning involved in using the Internet to research the history and culture of African Americans presents far more of a challenge for both parents and children than passively watching a television.

My youngest son, like other adolescents, is fascinated by rap music and has learned to "lay beats" on a computer, which is both creative and challenging. This investigative and inquisitive behavior should be cultivated at younger ages and can be a project for Birthing Circles that can continue to provide educational support for the child as he enters the summer of his life. Cooperative computer purchases are already taking place in black neighborhoods around the country, and civic and religious groups can contribute to these purchases as part of their outreach to these communities.

In 1985, I was instrumental in establishing the Computer Institute for Teaching Youth (CITY) in the Preston Taylor Homes, a public housing project in Nashville. For a leasing fee of $1 per year, the local housing authority allowed us to renovate a burned-out unit and convert it into an after-school program of linked computers, thanks to a generous donation from United Press International for staff and computers. This was in the early days of computing, but the twelve machines were fairly powerful for their day; they became an instant hit among the residents as entertainment, education, and research tools.

Because parents were just as fascinated with the machines, we expanded the services and offered adult classes in word processing and spreadsheet management. A club called I Believe in Myself (IBIM for short) was started for boys and girls in their summer years, and was done purely to enhance the self-esteem of the children. Attendance was mandatory in order to work on the computers, and the students rarely missed a class. We taught the children about the rich scientific contributions of such persons as Charles Drew, Lewis Latimer, Mae Jemison, and other black scientists who distinguished themselves in many areas.

The teachers in the program were excited about the flexibility they had in teaching, and the children loved it all. Though it lasted only two years, its impact was substantial and far ranging. And no one even missed television during the classes.

Committed teachers and parents who want the best for black boys can do this by engaging in a simple "technological transfer" represented by a move away from the television and to the computer. The Internet can act as an electronic drum for the global African community. In fact, in 1995 it was instrumental in organizing the Million Man March.

More recently, it has served as one of the best tools for educating people about the cases of Mumia Abu-Jamal, Abner Louima, and Amadou Diallo. In the work I do, I find that young black males in their summer years are eager to work on computers. They are particularly attracted to the idea of communicating with people around the world. Chart 7 shows some of the sobering statistics, which show why it is vital that all African Americans, particularly African-American children, have knowledge in and access to computers and the Internet: A child in a low-income white family is three times more likely to have Internet access as a child in a comparable black family and four times more likely than a Latino child. In families earning between $15,000 and $35,000, 33 percent of whites have computers in the home, but only 19 percent of blacks do.

Blacks should think of the technological gap as *partially* a self-help project. The affordability of computers today actually makes it more cost-effective to own a computer than not; renting computer time or traveling to facilities that have free computer access is time-consuming. Furthermore, purchasing goods over the Internet can also save money that would otherwise be spent at traditional brick-and-mortar stores. Educators, policy makers, and parents could mount a "Marshall Plan" to ensure that by 2010 this technological gap will be eliminated and that the Young Warriors in their summer years can continue to beat

**CHART 7: PERCENT OF HOMES HAVING COMPUTERS
BY ETHNICITY**

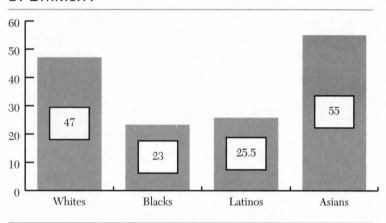

Source: U.S. Commerce Department, 1999 Report, "Falling Through the Net"

the electronic drum. It can begin with all black organizations—civic, professional, and religious—purchasing and donating ten fully equipped state-of-the-art computers to black families each year for the next ten years.

Conservatively, this could place a hundred thousand computers in black homes each year, and over a million by the year 2010. The donation program should include payment for one year of Internet access and maintenance contracts with vendors until each family is familiar with the basic maintenance of the system.

Black organizations can decide for themselves how the ten computers can be distributed, perhaps through contests, raffles, or incentive programs. Some organizations will be able to place more, but none should place less than ten per year. This program will do much to aid African-American families to keep pace with the technological revolution currently under way.

Mental Health and Black Boys

When the mental health of black boys is discussed, it usually focuses on two areas: intelligence and violence. From saliva to bell curves, the physiological analysis of black males creates the impression of a genetic predisposition to violence and a lack of intelligence. In 1999, the University of Chicago reported a widely cited study in which cortisol, a stress hormone, was noticeably low in the saliva of aggressive boys between the ages of seven and twelve. Though the study had only thirty-eight subjects, it was seen as a "breakthrough" in understanding how to treat violent youth; one of the researchers, Keith McBurnett, concluded, "Perhaps what we're dealing with here is a biological propensity that's resistant to treatment, which is very troubling. The implication is that we may need to discard our traditional notions of treatment with these kids in favor of trying to help them fit in and find a niche in society where their aggressiveness and lack of a sense of danger is an asset." Once again, black males as inferior and aggressive is suggested. If aggressive behavior is biological, as this terribly flawed study suggests, then it stands to reason that black boys in their summer years are hopelessly unresponsive to counseling and other interventions.

Robert Guthrie, in his book *Even the Rat Was White* shows how the patterns of making young black children feel inferior have been a part of "scholarly" research since the beginning of educational investigations in this country. While most social scientists consider themselves free of racist worldviews, in a 1997 article in *Educational Researcher*, James Scheurich and Michelle Young argue that "epistemological racism" pervades the research involving persons of color. They opine that it arises out of racism's domination of society, and that a "white" world-view is simply taken for granted by most scientists. The denial that a "white worldview" exists among most white scientists manifests itself when journals not accepted "by the mainstream" are viewed with contempt by those who evaluate black scholars for tenure. This epistemological racism forces black scholars to adopt strategies for surviving the academy that comprises what they may actually know to be true about black populations. Publishing the "right stuff," or what one of my colleagues refers to as the "white stuff," is a necessary strategy for gaining tenure at most traditionally white universities. This biased research justified the enslavement of black people, preserved the notion that racial segregation was the best way to educate all children, and supported the idea that white genetic pools would be contaminated with the addition of intellectually inferior black blood. The invention of the "intelligence test" forced psychology to give up its political virginity and began the consignment of black children to lower educational castes. Guthrie sites the infamous early-twentieth-century crusade of Stanford University psychologist Lewis Terman, who convinced several state legislatures to sterilize men, women, and children who were deemed "moronic" based on intelligence test data. Over ten thousand persons were sterilized during the Terman years, with many of them poor, black, retarded, and consigned to the netherworld of state mental hospitals.

While black violence and genetic inferiority seem to dominate the comparative literature between black and white boys, what is rarely discussed is the difference in mental health issues between these two groups. Random schoolyard shootings and white-on-white crime have recently illuminated the instability of white boys' mental health. The Centers for Disease Control notes that:

Current data confirms previous research that showed a dif-
ferential vulnerability to psychological disorders for boys
as compared with girls. . . . Several researchers suggest
that boys' greater susceptibility to such problems may be
explained to psychosocial stressors in their environments,
such as family conflict, divorce and parental psychopathol-
ogy. . . . Moreover, according to parental reports, higher
proportion of white children have had one or more of
these disorders than Asian or black children. . . .

The study also said,

*It is surprising that the prevalence of these disorders was
not higher for minority children because black and His-
panic families have several characteristics that suggest
they are at risk for higher rates of psychological disorders.*
[Italics added]

This is an important finding despite the fact that the
researchers seem surprised that black and Latino children do
not suffer from mental disorders as much as their white peers.
Similar to the reaction to the higher incidence of birth defects
among white infants, there seems to be a reluctance to discuss
the psychological problems associated with being young, white,
and male. Violence continues to be associated with being young
and black, despite the frequency of the mass shootings perpe-
trated by white boys in recent years. Parents, educators, or anyone involved with black boys need to understand such
information to counterbalance the negative image of black boys
during their summer years.

Young Warriors Councils

In recent years, Boys and Girls Clubs, the Boy Scouts, and several other organizations have become more "culturally sensitive" to the needs of our sons. The Boy Scouts of America, for example, now gives a merit badge for "crime prevention," indicating its "cultural awareness" that some of its members live in high-crime areas. Nearly all of these organizations have Black History Month programs, recognize the birthday of Martin Luther King Jr., and in some cases celebrate Kwanzaa. At best, however, these activities are grafted onto the association's programs. They are peripheral rather than central to the needs of the black boys within the organization. What black boys need are clubs and organizations that are culturally specific to them.

The Birthing Circle should continue until the boy is five years old, at which time he should be inducted into a Young Warrior Council. These clubs are modeled on the Poro Societies of West Africa.

Poro Societies removed their initiates from their homes so that they would be immersed in their training. The boys memorized the history and laws of their clan and of surrounding clans. One of the more accurate moments of the film *Amistad* was Cinque's helping in his own legal defense. This was a core teaching of Poro students—learn and understand the law of others as well as your own. Boys learned the medicinal properties of plants for a range of ailments, and studied the literature of their clan and other great legendary traditions of West Africa. They learned as many languages as they could, again reflected in Cinque's relatively quick mastery of English before his trial.

The Young Warriors Council expand the six months to eight years the time devoted to the boys' psychological, social, physical, and emotional development. This lengthy period is necessary because, unlike with Poro Society, black boys are returned to environments that hinder their development, not support it. *Protecting* a child is different from *overprotecting* a child, and black boys remain vulnerable to racism as they mature more than white boys. The steps in creating Young Warriors Councils are outlined below. These ideas are based on discussions with dozens of educators and hundreds of black boys, which I have conducted for many years. I have deliberately made them flexible so that they can be adopted by a variety of organizations.

1. *The Birthing Circle established during pregnancy should surround the child until five years of age.* Birthing Circles should continue the attention given to the mother and child during pre- and postnatal care throughout the boy's spring years. Each Birthing Circle should be given a name, including the area in which the mother lives, the street name, and her family name. For example, the Birthing Circle for the son of Mary Williams, who lives on Malcolm X Boulevard in Harlem, would be called: Harlem-Malcolm X/Williams Birthing Circle. Seven Birthing Circles together would comprise a *clan*, which will help govern the lives of seven boys from conception to age five, and eventually will form the Young Warriors Councils that take over when the seven boys turn five. Birthing Circles can continue to "adopt" other women and boys who wish to be in them, and the members of the circle should keep detailed records of the women and children throughout the life of the child. This latter point is similar to Poro Societies, which kept meticulous records of past

students so that the clan history could be passed down from generation to generation.

2. *At five years old, the boys begin the process of becoming members of the Young Warriors Council.* Seven boys should be inducted in a ceremony that announces their admittance to the council. The ceremony should be attended by as many family members as possible, during which the following program occurs:

   a. Pouring of libations to the ancestors. This ceremony has become increasingly popular at African-centered gatherings; water is poured over a plant or directly on the ground to pay homage to the ancestors. Ironically, the use of liquor to do the same thing has become a popular means of paying tribute to "dead homies" in inner cities throughout the nation. Libations signify the connection of all African people in the *Maafa*, and of the respect the living have for the dead, as well as for the unborn. It should be done by the oldest male and female present to symbolize the importance of both genders in the life of the Young Warrior.

   b. Greetings by the oldest woman in the Birthing Circle. After the libations are completed, the sacredness of the woman in African culture should be acknowledged with the oldest woman opening the program. This is a simple yet important announcement to the gathering that women give birth to the world, and that without them all life would cease. It also reminds the young boy that women are to be listened to and respected. Members of the Birthing Circle should review nostalgic incidents so that the young man can hear how his elders have cared for him since his conception.

c. Greetings by the oldest man in the Birthing Circle. The presence of the elder man is important since it is a ceremony involving male initiation, and he should speak words concerning the importance of boys, and give a brief history of the Birthing Circle.

d. Reading of the *Nguzo Saba* (Seven Principles) by the mother of the boy. The widely known *Nguzo Saba* (pronounced nah-gu-ZSO SAH-bah), read by the mother to her son, emphasizes how these have been and should continue to be guiding principles in his life. Created by Maulana Karenga in 1965, the *Nguzo Saba* has found popularity among African Americans as the celebration of Kwanzaa becomes more widespread. Maulana Karenga stresses the importance of informality in its celebration. The principle, though elaborated on by several persons, are originally stated as follows:

1. *Umoja* (uu-MOH-jah) Unity: To strive for and maintain unity in the family, community, nation, and race.

2. *Kujichagulia* (KUU´-jee-chah-guu-lee-ah) Self-Determination: To define ourselves, name ourselves, create for ourselves, and speak for ourselves.

3. *Ujima* (uu-JEE´-mah) Collective Work and Responsibility: To build and maintain our community together and make our brother's and sister's problems our problems and to solve them together.

4. *Ujamaa* (UU´-jah-mah) Cooperative Economics: To build and maintain our own stores, shops, and other businesses and to profit from them together.

5. *Nia* (NEE´-ah) Purpose: To make our collective vocation the building and developing of our community in order to restore our people to their traditional greatness.

6. *Kuumba* (Ku-UUM´-bah) Creativity: To do always as much as we can, in the way we can, in order to leave our community more beautiful and beneficial than we inherited it.

7. *Imani* (eh-MAH´-NEE) Faith: To believe with all our heart in our people, our parents, our teachers, our leaders, and the righteousness and victory of our struggle.

e. Recitation of the *Nguzo Saba* by each of the seven boys being inducted. The seven boys repeat the reading of the *Nguzo Saba* for emphasis.

f. Gift by the oldest man of a strip of *Kente* cloth to each boy, which will signify his induction into the Young Warriors Council. *Kente* cloth has become symbolic of the beauty and strength of West African culture. The cloth is both beautiful and strong, and as each boy receives his strip, the elder should note its beauty and strength in relation to him. Just as European coats of arms are visible representations of a family's history, so *Kente* represents the culture, art, history, and folklore of clans in West Africa. The Young Warriors Council should adopt a *Kente* cloth, agreed upon by the elders, which reflects the boys within the council. Each cloth should be worn at appropriate gatherings and, when not in use, hung in a prominent place in the boy's bedroom.

g. Seven boys stand together while members of the Birthing Circle form an unbroken circle around them. The oldest man, the youngest man, the oldest woman, and the youngest woman in the Birthing Circle then offer prayers for the well-being of the boys as well as the members of the Birthing Circle. At the end of this ritual, the Birthing Circle is renamed the Young Warriors Council, and the seven Young Warriors are officially inducted.

h. All persons engage in a community feast (*karamu*), which consists of healthy food and no alcohol. Kwanzaa celebrations are also ended with a *karamu*, and the feast gives the boys and the members of the Young Warriors Council an opportunity to bond even further. Since there are minors present, no alcohol should be served, which also reminds the boys of the importance of avoiding substances harmful to the body.

The Birthing Circle has now become the Young Warriors Council and the boys, who are now five years old, should have several structured pursuits that prepare them for school.

3. The fifth year should include the following activities:
   a. Monthly meetings for members of the Young Warriors Council and the seven Young Warriors should be informal and rotate among the homes of council members. The meetings, a continuation of the Birthing Circle, should supplement the education received by the boy in his formal schooling. Run on a rotating basis by the parents/guardians of each of the seven boys, meetings should begin by addressing council business.

   Group activities, which should remain flexible, should center the boys' attention on their place in the adult world, and take into account the preferences of the adults and the boys.

   b. Each of the seven Young Warriors should read three age-appropriate books during the first year. Reading should by now be a habit with the boys, and book selection should create group cohesiveness around a topic of interest. The boys should agree on the books they collectively read and discuss why they chose them. The elders in the council should guide the boys in selecting their books after listening to the boys' suggestions. Black Books Galore (http://www.blackbooksgalore.com/bbgthirt.html.) is an excellent place to select books for black children.

c. The newly formed Young Warriors Council should take field trips, discuss healthy living, and provide science instruction and lectures that teach the boys about African history and culture. Young Warriors Councils may choose to exchange information among themselves about supplemental education, but the burden of instruction for its boys should rest with each individual Young Warriors Council. Similar activities were conducted during Poro initiation, when boys were taught extensively about astronomy, agriculture, art, and music.

d. At the end of twelve months, the Young Warriors Council should conduct an agreed-upon ceremony that inducts the boys into their Sixth Year. No set ceremony is offered for this event; rather, it should be planned by all council members as an exercise in creativity. It should showcase what the Young Warriors have learned during the year.

4. The sixth year should repeat the basic curriculum of the fifth year, adding information technology as a key component of the learning process. While the addition of computers and the Internet can begin during the fifth year, it should be formalized when the boys turn six. The ubiquity of computers does not automatically translate into computer literacy. The Young Warriors should be thoroughly familiar with the use of computers by the end of their sixth year. If adults within the council are weak in this area, they should involve themselves in learning about using new technology. If computers are unavailable in the homes of the council members, efforts

should be made to hold a portion of the monthly meetings at a local library or other facility where Internet access is available. A group project may involve purchasing computers with a year's access to the Internet for each of the Young Warriors. Council elders should emphasize using technology to establish close ties with Africa and the *Maafa*. Many resources exist on the Internet that make it easy to locate "pen pals" among African children, particularly in West, East, and South Africa.

Spelling bees and oratorical contests should be held among the seven Young Warriors and their councils. Spelling bees are old-fashioned ways of honing spelling skills while having fun. A few years ago, I helped organize a spelling bee for a local civic group whose officers were skeptical about whether it would attract a large crowd. Each family of club members offered their best speller, and they were divided into appropriate age categories. Words were selected by a panel of three teachers who were members of the group. Prizes for each age group included a dictionary, a desk encyclopedia, a thesaurus, and a book on black history. Attendance was excellent at the event, and several people commented on how simple yet fun preparing for the contest was. It brought families closer together and rewarded good study habits. Oratorical contests, in which contestants select passages to recite and are then judged by a panel, are good ways of increasing the public-speaking ability of black children. Relatively easy events to organize, they can be held in churches or community centers. Debates are also in keeping with Poro Society initiation rites. All members of Poro Society were taught the importance of public speaking. Witnesses at the trial of Joseph Cinque noted his eloquence, even though he spoke with broken English, about his desire for freedom.

5. The seventh year begins the study of law and media. If the proper instruction has taken place during the first two years of the Young Warriors program, the seven Warriors will be prepared to analyze their self-image by understanding how the world sees them. The first six years of the boys' lives should be a time in which there is no lack of positive black male role models, something that psychologist Carolyn Murray of the University of California at Riverside says is the most critical element of the development of self-image among black boys. The Young Warrior Councils should surround the boys with older black males who can mentor them and serve as their surrogate fathers in case no fathers are present in the boys' immediate families. They can help to teach the boys about how black males are perceived in media and how these perceptions begin when the boys are young. Black children watch a lot of television; teaching them to recognize how their images are manufactured, manipulated, and marketed is a critical learning experience for them.

The boys must also become familiar with the law, particularly laws related to arrest and incarceration. I am angry that I have to write this because of the numerous police shootings involving police and black males. Ideally, six-year-old black boys should be focused on their education and the things that youngsters do at this age. Their environment should be relatively free from worries that they might be stopped and killed by police officers. This is not the case, however, and Young Warriors must learn simple lessons like these as they approach adolescence.

Classes should be held with workers in juvenile facilities, and attorneys who have experience with youth law should talk to the seven Warriors. They should talk frankly with boys about what happens to them if the police stop them. If possible, Young Warriors should visit juvenile courts to witness firsthand the legal process. Black boys are being criminalized at increasingly younger ages, and six is not too young to hear why this is so.

The legal instruction should not be tedious; mock trials could acquaint the boys with the role of law-enforcement officers. Most local law schools and/or dedicated lawyers can help arrange legal instruction quite easily if approached by a conscientious group of parents wanting the best for their sons. Two mock trials that give roles to lawyers, judges, and juries can be held during the year. The National Bar Association is a good place to seek help in this effort.

Visits with responsible black police officers should be done carefully. Young Warriors and the members of the Warriors Council should question the police, particularly in the area of how law enforcement works in their neighborhood. In light of police homicides and brutality cases in the past few years, e.g., Cincinnati, I have found police departments eager to participate in events that invite them to discuss their work as law enforcers. Many cities have organized black police officer groups that are often at odds with their departments over the treatment of ethnic citizens. A visit by officers on a twice-yearly basis, particularly just before winter vacation and summer vacation, is a good investment in the safety of black boys.

6. The seventh and eighth years should expand on what the Young Warriors have already learned, particularly in the areas of media and law. In addition, Council members should be aware of negative images confronting black boys in entertainment. Older parents who disparage rap should understand that younger black males identify strongly with rap artists. Lil' Bow Wow, a thirteen-year-old rapper and the protégé of

Snoop Dog, has lyrics that reinforce the image that little boys are "dawgs." He joins the list of black boy artists who have demeaning names such as Another Bad Creation. Black parents and adults in the Young Warriors Council must educate *themselves* about hip-hop culture and rap music.

Young Warriors Councils should also include an expanded curriculum centering on music and the arts of African people. Jazz and music from the *Maafa* can be used to extend the listening range of the boys. Books such as *The New Grove Dictionary of Jazz* are extremely helpful in choosing music that can be used for *black* music appreciation classes. Young Warriors should hear classic jazz artists such as Jelly Roll Morton, Louis Armstrong, Billie Holiday, and Miles Davis; and council members who know about the history of jazz should hold lectures. Again, community resources should always be utilized if resources are not available within the council. If members of the circle lack extensive knowledge about the history of black American music, then they should find someone outside of the council to help.

It is particularly important that a history of black music be traced from Africa to America. Portia Maultsby's research at Indiana University on the evolution of black music styles is helpful in visualizing the history of music from both sides of the Atlantic. There should be a discussion on how Elvis Presley, the Rolling Stones, Eric Clapton, and others borrowed heavily from the blues tradition for their inspiration, teaching black boys to appreciate the influence their ancestors have had on music throughout the *Maafa*. Analyzing the history of blues, gospel, jazz, rock and roll, rhythm and blues, soul, and rap will be fun for all in the council and at the same time infuse everyone with a positive sense of self and an appreciation of the cultural contributions of African Americans.

By this point, Young Warriors should be reading and discussing four books per year. Consulting reading lists from black bookstores and getting recommendations by word of mouth can help. Books should be discussed informally, and each boy should be encouraged to participate. If a hearing- or seeing-impaired boy is a Young Warrior, provisions should be made for interpreters or any other services to allow for his full participation. The adults in the council should ask questions that will spark discussions of the book by the boys. Max Rodriguez, Angel Rasbury, and Carol Taylor's *Sacred Fire* provides a list of the one hundred books that *all* African Americans should read, while Haki Madhubuti's *Black Men: Obsolete, Single, Dangerous?* gives a list of two hundred books that all black people should read. This combined list provides a solid base for beginning a systematic reading of black life in the *Maafa*. I hesitate to list a "canon" of black books, since I believe that individual Young Warriors Councils should develop their own reading lists relevant to the boys they are mentoring. Some children can understand books such as *Before the Mayflower*, which outlines the contributions of Africans to the ancient world before others. What is exciting about a systematic reading program is that parents, teachers, and children are involved in lively discussions that will be mentally engaging and informative.

Field trips should be expanded to include concerts and other venues where black art is showcased. Many historically black colleges and universities (HBCUs) host regular groups of black middle and high school students from all over the country, giving tours of black campuses and historic sites in the South. These trips give visual connections to the sites where enslavement of our ancestors occurred and even more important sites where struggles against racism took place.

Suggestions for places to visit can be found in George Cantor's *Historic Landmarks of Black America*. They should include the traditional visits to Martin Luther King's grave in Atlanta and also some of the following sites:

Vicksburg, Mississippi—slave auction sites

Sea Islands of Georgia—Gullah cultural historic sites

Tuskegee University, Tuskegee, Alabama—site of the laboratory of George Washington Carver

Fisk University—Aaron Douglass murals; histories of W. E. B. Du Bois, George Padmore, Nikki Giovanni, and the Fisk Jubilee Singers

Harlem, New York

Preservation Hall, New Orleans—"ground zero" for a history of jazz

Underground railroad stations, particularly in Ohio

Du Sable Museum, Chicago—one of the best African-American museums in the country

Piney Woods School, Piney Woods, Mississippi—one of the best secondary schools in the country with a history of black education to match

Southampton County, Virginia—site of the 1831 Nat Turner rebellion against enslavement

Nicodemus, Kansas—one of the oldest black settlements in America

This is a short list of historic places that are often passed over for more popular sites. Money should never be a hindrance to exploring cultural sites within the community of the Young Warriors Councils. Black communities throughout the United States have cultural histories that are often unknown to their residents. Furthermore, several of these sites exist in white neighborhoods, particularly in suburban areas that are now predominantly white. Burial grounds of enslaved Africans have been discovered in New York and in Nashville with neither in proximity to local black communities, and have been fruitful in understanding the early cultural legacy of Africans in America. Within the vicinity of each council, scavenger hunts and historical documentation of black people's contribution should be researched as the boys grow older. Parents and council members can coordinate them. These can be viewed as "sacred spaces" in our communities and would provide places of visitation and meditation for our children.

7. The ninth and tenth years are critical in the development of Young Warriors. For most boys this is the fourth grade, when the assault on their psychological well-being begins in earnest. I have speculated earlier why these assaults intensify at the beginning of puberty, and it is important that the elders in the Warriors Councils become vigilant in monitoring the institutions that are instructing their boys. Councils that have already established strong ties with the seven Young Warriors' school should strengthen these ties. The Council should make sure that parents attend all parent-teacher conferences and, when possible, should volunteer as teachers' aides in the Young Warriors' classrooms. Research is overwhelming that a close tie to the school by parents ensures good grades and strong attendance; this should be a primary concern of Young Warriors Councils.

   The seven Warriors should also be included in the ceremonies marking the induction of new Young Warriors. Their participation can consist of pouring libations or simply attending the ceremonies. During these special occasions, the boys should wear their *Kente* cloth strips, and their parents should encourage peer mentoring between the older and younger Warriors.

8. The eleventh and twelfth years are looking-ahead years for the rites-of-passage ceremony, celebrating the seven Young Warriors' turning thirteen. By now, they should be reading five books per year, have a broad understanding of their legal rights, have a worldview of African life, and have a firm understanding of computers and the Internet. The emphasis during these years is a strong education in savings and economics. The seven Young Warriors may already be earning and managing money, but now the boys should be taught the global dimensions of money, economies, and thrift. How money can be used to strengthen black communities (*Ujamaa* in the *Nguzo Saba*) should be taught and encouraged. If they have not already done so, Young Warriors should open savings accounts in each of their names, preferably at a black financial institution.

It is also not too early to teach lessons in how Eurocentric institutions handle money. The Young Warriors and the councils can both benefit from learning how Wall Street and foreign financial markets operate to ensure that the institutions, corporations, and countries they represent stay strong and healthy, often at the expense of persons of color. Mock investment is a way of doing this, and friendly competition between Warriors Councils can be set up, with simulated investments on Wall Street. Various on-line trading sites such as etrade.com offer investment simulations that teach youngsters how the stock market works. Simulations should always be conducted with an eye toward teaching young men the importance of reinvesting their money within the African-American community.

At a very real level, each council should begin an investment club where the Young Warriors' money, small though it may be, is invested to earn returns in cooperative ventures. The councils can advise the boys about investment possibilities, cooperative investment, and other projects that involve the money they have saved and lent to the club. Small contributions of $2 per week by each Young Warrior can result in an annual investment of over $700. Like other activities of the Young Warriors Council, advice should be taken from experts in the particular area of group interest. If available, black stockbrokers or any expert in long-term financial management, can advise the group. The council should be particularly concerned about college tuition for the boys. Many states have government-run tuition plans to lighten the financial burden of parents sending children to college. Again, the council should base the amount of the investment on the economic level of its community. The group should unanimously agree upon the amount so that its financial goals can be met. The investment club should continue into the autumn years of the Young Warriors.

The goal of the investment clubs is not to encourage the materialism that characterizes much of the West, but to teach the boys about the system that influences so many young black men to sacrifice everything in the pursuit of money. Understanding how economies work and making them beneficial to African-American communities should be the goal of the councils during this year. Niki Butler's *The New Color of Success* is one of the few books that discusses young black entrepreneurs and how they acquired their money. What is refreshing about the book is that it *does not* include athletes and entertainers, and it provides a new array of young and rich black folk with goals that largely have to do with their commitment to African-centered values.

The end of the twelfth year marks the beginning of the rite of passage that will induct the seven Young Warriors into adulthood.

6

The Seasons of Our Sons: Autumn, Ages 13–21

I have told you all these things . . . because you are my son, the eldest of my sons, and because I have nothing to hide from you. There is a certain form of behavior to observe, and certain ways of acting in order that the guiding spirit of our race may approach you also.

—CAMARA LAYE, GUINEAN AUTHOR OF *THE BLACK CHILD*

The Notion of "Adolescence"

I would there were no age between three and three and twenty, or that youth would sleep out the rest; for there is nothing in the between but getting wenches with child, wronging the ancientry, stealing and fighting

—SHAKESPEARE, *THE WINTER'S TALE*, III, III

"Adolescence" is a nebulous Latin term that literally means "to be nourished." It's defined by the hip *Encarta* dictionary as the period preceding adulthood in *human beings*. An interesting definition, particularly since the only animals we apply this term to are humans. There are no "teenage lions" or "adolescent zebras," only humans have created what playwright Eugene O'Neill once called "Ah, Wilderness." A more empirical definition would mark its beginning at puberty, which is often marked by the beginning of wet dreams for boys and menarche for girls. Puberty is said to end at the age of twenty-one. Neither definition is completely accurate; college attendance can postpone entry into adulthood, and dropping out of school can accelerate maturity. In an effort toward simplification, a friend of mine says that you become an adult when you fill out your own tax forms and no one claims you on theirs. Three things *are* certain, though, about "adolescence": 1) no one knows exactly when it begins, 2) no one knows exactly when it ends, and 3) our understanding of it is determined by shifting social values, e.g., legal drinking age, and political events such as boys' suddenly becoming the "few good men" needed to fight a nation's wars.

Educators mark the beginning of *formalized adolescence* with the onset of the Industrial Revolution, since entry into the labor market by children was considered unethical and eventually unlawful. In no place is adolescence more formalized than in the United States, where an entire group of young people renamed "slackers" or "Gen-Xers" have earned representational status as adolescents. Adolescence was a way of allowing the youngster to mark time and prepare for the adult world of work. Institutions sprang up that supported this notion, such as high school college-preparatory classes, summer camps, and the Boy Scouts. For middle-class youngsters, the period allowed for working in their fathers' businesses, completing internships, and participating in other creative money-making endeavors. For poorer, young working-class people, it was a period of idleness that was broken up by temporary menial work that was virtually disconnected from career planning. Instead, opportunities abounded for adolescents, particularly adolescent boys, to engage in what would be known by the mid-twentieth century as "juvenile delinquency," and the association of crime with adolescence became established and persists to the present day.

But there are groups in which antisocial behavior is not the norm but the exception. Crime, and specifically homicide, among Jewish adolescents is low, as it is for Muslims, Mormons, and fundamentalist Christians—groups that stress service and parochial education. In 1995, F. Landis MacKellar and Machiko Yanagishita's *Homicide in the United States: Who's at Risk?* found that African Americans had the highest homicide rate for the period from 1989 to 1991 (38.8 victims per 100,000), followed by Hispanics (15.5), American Indians (11.7), whites (5.7), and Asian Americans (5.5). Homicide rates for persons of color have fallen substantially since the early 1970s, narrowing the racial gap. Nonwhite homicide rates, which were ten times higher than those of whites in the early 1970s, are now six to seven times higher. They also found the persons who were at greatest risk of being murdered are young adults, representing three-fifths of all victims; males, representing three-quarters of all victims; and African Americans, representing half of all victims. According to the Sentencing Project statistics, it is actually young black males who are far more likely to be murdered than any other segment of the population.

Homicide rates are highest for young adults in their twenties, but for the first time, the rate for men ages twenty to twenty-four exceeded the rate for men ages twenty-five to twenty-nine. Although the rates for men in their early twenties are high, (18 per 100,000 for white men, and 127 per 100,000 for nonwhite men), they are well below the record highs set by the baby-boom generation in the 1970s and 1980s. But this trend reverses itself for younger age groups. Rates for teenage boys are now at record highs. For nonwhite males ages fifteen to nineteen, homicide rates in 1990 were 92 per 100,000, and for whites, only 13 per 100,000. Significantly, homicide rates for black male teen-agers more than doubled between 1985 and 1990.

The researchers also found that violence is increasing among the very young. Rates in 1990 for preschoolers (up to age four) rose to their highest levels in forty years for all race-gender groups. Homicide rates of minority preschoolers increased by roughly one-third between 1985 and 1990.

Finally, for most adults age forty and older, the risk of being a homicide victim declined over the past decade. Rates in 1990 are lower than those in 1980 for almost all age, gender, and racial groups. The only group to experience an increased risk is non-white elderly women (ages seventy-five and older). Homicide offenders, like victims, tend to be young and male. The majority (52 percent) of offenders are between the ages of fifteen and twenty-four. Over half (56 percent) are black.

Rites of Passage

Poverty and drug abuse are not necessarily strong predictors of homicidal behavior, even though they appear to be connected. If this were the case, American Indians would have the highest rate of these behaviors, since alcoholism and poverty are at peak levels in that population. What American Indians and other groups have in common are traditions and rituals that formally induct their sons into adulthood. These rites of passage occur at various times in the life cycle, and include baptism, consecra-tion, weddings, and funerals. All cultures create ceremonies to mark these life transitions with ceremonial rituals, in which fam-ilies and friends of the initiate participate.

The most visible of these is the bar mitzvah ceremony, when

Jewish boys are initiated into manhood at the age of thirteen. The phrase "bar mitzvah" literally translated is "son command-ment," and implies that the boy has a thorough understanding of Jewish law and is formally accepted as a man who participates in the life of the Jewish community. "Adolescence," while used to describe Jewish boys, is subordinated to the ritual of bar mitz-vah. The Jewish *community*—rather than driver's license bureaus, the selective service system, or state legislatures—decides when a boy becomes a man. As with other rites of pas-sage, the ceremony takes place in front of community members to reinforce group cohesion and to pass rituals down from one generation to another.

Rites-of-passage ceremonies in the African-American com-munity were disrupted by the period of enslavement. Slowly, the rituals associated with Poro Society were forgotten and replaced by ceremonies taken directly from American culture, which had no relevance to the culture of Africans in the *Maafa*. Cotillions for girls—still being held among members of what E. Franklin Frazier derisively referred to as the "black bourgeoisie"—imi-tate what is perceived as being elements of European culture.

Such alienation from African culture is most destructive when it comes to rites-of-passage ceremonies for boys; these rit-uals define the very essence of what birth, adulthood, marriage, and death mean to the culture. Transition to adulthood is con-sidered the most important passage because it tells the boy what his responsibilities are to himself and to his community. The absence of adolescent rites of passage has made it difficult for black boys to know when they become men. Linked with the absence of role models, black boys have arbitrarily defined man-hood in ways that are often destructive. Fathering babies, carry-ing a gun, selling drugs, and having sex, while not peculiar to African-American culture, are nevertheless viewed by many alienated black youth as appropriate indicators of manhood. While racist media exaggerate much of this macho behavior, it exists in varying degrees among young black males. A young black male once told me that he considered buying a "Glock 26, as opposed to a 19," as being a definite "sign of being a man." I knew what a Glock was, but I was surprised that the fourteen-year-old could distinguish the models. I told him that neither of them made him a man. He asked me what did. I paused and told him the ability to take care of himself and others. He liked that idea, and our conversation ended far better than it had begun.

Rob

Rob, a young black male, wanted to see me because he needed to talk about his explosive anger. I would later find out that even though he was only fifteen years old, he had been physically abusive to two previous girlfriends. I very much wanted to meet this young man, partly because it is very unusual for an adolescent African-American male to *ask* for counseling. Stanley Sue's classic study of who uses mental health centers indicates that black males are the least likely to seek mental health treatment, preferring instead to talk with trusted friends or "keep their feelings to themselves."

The next day, at precisely the appointed time, Rob walked into my office, introduced himself, and started asking questions even before he'd sat down. His anxiety was obvious, and he wanted to know what I knew about him. I told him that I knew he had an "anger management problem," and he queried whether that was all I knew. I assured him that it was, and only then did he settle in his seat; his eyes darted around my office as

if to absorb anything he could that would expand his understanding of me.

I asked him how he felt, and he immediately responded,
"Mad."

"About what?" I asked.

"Everything," he replied.

I asked him if he was angry about coming to see me, and he
said no, deliberately leading him into a contradiction of what he
just said.

He got the point, smiled, and said, "I guess it ain't *everything*,
is it?"

I smiled in return and told him that, like any other emotion,
anger can usually be ranked on a scale of one to ten, depending
on what is being discussed. As if anticipating my next question,
he asked me to name some things, and he would give the degree
to which he was angry about them, using my scale, with ten
being "extremely."

I said, "Job."

He answered, "Six."

I said, "Girlfriend."

He answered, "Eight."

I said, "Oldest brother."

He answered, "Seven."

I said, "Mother."

He answered, "Twenty."

Wanting to stop there but also wanting to get a broader picture of his rage, I supplied him with a list of words, and his
responses clearly showed an enormous amount of fury toward
his family, particularly his parents. After a few minutes, I asked
him if he noticed a trend, and he replied, somewhat sarcastically,
that he didn't need a list to know that and that he could have told

me that without my little test. He had become extremely angry, and he ranted about why people ask so many questions and many other things that were only barely related to what we had been discussing. I asked him why was he angry. Stopping short, his mouth still open, he looked at me and said he did not know. I didn't respond. We both sat there in silence for a few moments until he suddenly burst into tears. I was stunned. Things were happening far quicker than I had imagined they would, and as I handed him a tissue from my desk, I asked him a question that normally would not be asked for many counseling sessions.

"Why do you hate your mother so much?" I asked.

"Because she didn't protect me," he answered immediately.

"Against what?" I queried, disbelieving the speed at which this moment had arrived.

As the ensuing silence engulfed us, I knew that the next words would either be a total lie or an extremely painful truth. Rob said nothing for the next few minutes as he cried softly. I was determined not to break the silence, regardless of how long it took. After a few more moments had passed, he looked up at me and said, "Me being raped in my backyard."

Had I expected this response? No. But had he been a young woman, I might have. I knew that part of my not making the connection was sexist, and I was also surprised at how fast the first session had moved. Only ten minutes into the conference and I had already heard what usually takes days, weeks, or even months to hear.

There is always the possibility that a client is lying. Lying for effect, manipulation, protection, and sometimes for the sheer joy of lying. I also knew that instincts play an important role in counseling, particularly with Cinque's sons. Black men *will* lie to one another as all people lie, but I instinctively knew that Rob was not lying to me. His tears were real, and I knew that his anger and hurt were ready to be expressed and, hopefully, absolved.

I told Rob that what he had just done was probably the bravest thing that anyone could do. His tears were slowing down, and he looked at me, disregarding the recent dictum that black men should not look each other in the eyes. He said almost disbelievingly, "Really?" and I said yes and explained to him that all pain is real and that the pain he felt had come out in bad ways, but he was brave enough to move into himself and understand where his anger was. He breathed deeply, and unlike so many of my brothers who are waiting to explode and not exhale, he had chosen to deal with his anger at an early enough stage so that it would not consume him when he reached his winter years. Over the next weeks, we talked about anger, frustration, abandonment, rape, lies, fear, goodness, strength, and the many things that Claude Brown's menchildren talk about to very few people. Rob talked about how he was "fairly sure" that his mother knew that his male cousin had raped him, but it was unmentionable to anyone. The rapes were repeated during a three-year period, from the time Rob was eight until he was eleven, whenever there were visits from the twenty-something cousin. His guilt grew out of the fact that he felt he had begun to enjoy the brutal scenes; by the time he was ten, he thought that he was homosexual. His first experience with a girl was at eleven; when he told his cousin about this, the cousin suddenly stopped his molestations. His youthful promiscuity with girls, he believed, was in part due to his trying to bury the memories of his childhood. In all of this, he had kept the ugly secrets to himself, but he felt that his mother's strict attitude toward him was in part due to her blaming *him* for the sexual abuse. The burden of guilt, silence, fear, and anger had taken its toll on the young man, who was unsure about his manhood and where his anger was taking him.

Rob was no different from so many boys whom I have seen over the years, boys who are so confused by their anger that they take it out on whoever happens to be closest. The details of our sessions are not as important as the fact that Rob walked away from them renewed in his commitment to reject the temptations to "be hard" and the avoidance of discussions about the hurt, rage, confusion, and frustration he was feeling. His emotional reconciliation with his family took the form of telling his mother what had happened to him. She had absolutely no knowledge of what had happened to her son. Rob later told me that the tears she shed comforted him, and she told him that she loved him, which provided a bridge to a place where they could meet and learn to love and trust each other again.

Black Rage Revisited

I hesitated in presenting Rob's story at this point because it reinforces the image of "black rage" first discussed by William Grier and Price Cobbs in their 1968 book *Black Rage*. Published during the height of the urban rebellions of the 1960s and on the heels of Malcolm X's assassination, the book seemed the logical explanation for why black people in general, and black men in particular, were so angry. It was supposedly anchored in our inability to express this rage (anger turned inward) safely toward our oppressors. Their dubious psychoanalytic explanations (e.g., how much black women hate their hair, how black people make negative comments about their relatives ["the dozens"]), were quickly grasped by white persons seeking explanations for black anger. Grier and Cobbs were embraced as supporting the long-held notion that blacks were basically "angry" about nearly everything.

White psychiatrists such as Abram Kardiner and Lionel Ovesey in *Mark of Oppression* and prominent child psychiatrist Erik Erikson, whose racist classification of black identity was immortalized in his most influential book *Childhood and Society*, published fifty years ago, had offered earlier explanations of black anger:

> The babies of our colored countrymen . . . often receive sensual satisfactions which provide them with enough oral and sensory surplus for a lifetime, as clearly betrayed in the way they move, laugh, talk and sing. . . . Three identities are formed: (1) mammy's oral sensual "honey-child"—tender, expressive, rhythmical; (2) the evil identity of the dirty, anal sadistic, phallic-rapist "nigger"; and (3) the clean, anal-compulsive, restrained, friendly, but always sad "white man's Negro."

What is interesting about this strange classification of African Americans is that the book was and perhaps still is a widely accepted treatise for understanding black behavior from a psychoanalytic perspective. It reached its height as a "manual" for understanding black people during the 1960s, when it was carried in the knapsacks of white civil rights workers going south to "help" black people. Erikson was asked to purge this bit of racism in his text in the 1960 revision of the book, but he refused. *Childhood and Society* is now considered a "classic" in the field of developmental psychology.

Where would Rob fit into Erikson's categories? Nowhere. Black anger, though often analyzed, is rarely understood. It is viewed monolithically, with few nuances other than black boys directing their anger toward one another. I believe the obsession with black adolescent anger is an unconscious expression of white anxiety that it may one day be directed toward them. What if black adolescent menchildren today turned their guns from their inner-city brothers toward white suburbanites? What if the anger following the 1992 Rodney King decision in Los Angeles moved into Beverly Hills and Santa Monica? Derrick Bell, in his book *Faces at the Bottom of the Well*, talks about how racial themes are developed in America. Black men's lustful attitudes toward white women, the inferiority of black people, and the importance of symbolic gestures toward eliminating racism are a few. Black men killing other black men, a form of self-hate, is also one of them.

What if the self-hate turned into simple "hate" and was redirected toward whites? When the late African-American psychologist Bobby Wright was asked why blacks kill blacks, he replied that it was because they had not learned to kill whites. A macabre answer, but one that may be the prime motivation for research on black anger. Black men are taught to kill other black men through songs, books, and other people. Charles Silberman, author of *Criminal Justice, Criminal Violence*, expresses the anxiety regarding black anger. It is worth quoting him here at length:

> Blacks are no longer 'shy in their acts.' The poet Langston Hughes foresaw the change . . . in a bitterly sardonic poem he wrote when the great [black] tenor Roland Hayes was beaten by a white mob in Georgia:
>
> > *Negroes*
> > *Sweet and docile,*
> > *Meek, humble, and kind;*

> *Beware the day*
> *They change their mind.*
>
> *Wind*
> *In the cotton fields,*
> *Gentle breeze:*
> *Beware the hour*
> *It uproots trees!*

The change has come; blacks have changed their minds,
and more than trees are being uprooted. After 350 years of
fearing whites, black Americans have discovered that the
fear runs the other way, that whites are intimidated by
their very presence; it would be hard to overestimate what
an extraordinarily liberating force this discovery is. The
taboo against expression of anti-white anger is breaking
down, and 350 years of festering hatred has come spilling
out. [Italics added]

When it comes to black adolescents in their autumn years,
their understanding of this fear is virtually nonexistent. Most
adolescent black males do not understand how much whites fear
blacks, and they get in trouble because of this. Jim Myers, in his
book *Afraid of the Dark: What Whites and Blacks Need to Know*
About Each Other, opines that popular wisdom among African
Americans says that blacks must understand how whites fear
them and compensate for this:

> Whites are so often unsure of themselves that blacks rec-
> ognize they must approach the situation in ways that will
> put whites more at ease. In fact, there is a large body of
> conventional wisdom in black America about how to deal

with white people in ways that will not stir white fears. For example, it is said that you always have to tell white people what they want to hear; that it's not wise to let them know you have strong opinions or are knowledgeable about anything; or you must never let white people suspect they're not smart or in total control of the situation.

Black boys will eventually learn this, as do most blacks, and to the degree they do, they will navigate white institutions more or less easily. During the autumn years of black boys' lives, Young Warriors Councils must teach them this without compromising their integrity. Understanding white institutions is important, but the lesson should never come at the expense of personal integrity. "Selling out" is often a misused term among young brothers when applied to young black men who deal effectively with majority institutions. It *can* be used to describe black men who give unquestioning loyalty to systems who hurt them and their people.

White fear is expressed in many ways, such as the incredible police presence gathered to "keep the peace" when nearly 2 million black men gathered in Washington in October 1995. Hollywood is the best purveyor of this white fear of black anger. In *48 Hours*, Eddie Murphy's first film, there is the line, "I am your worst nightmare—a black man with a gun."

Black Adolescent Health

Health in adolescence is largely determined by the quality of health care received during childhood. Frequency of immunization, for example, varies significantly by race. Chart 8 shows that blacks and Latinos have the lowest immunization rates when

CHART 8: CHILDHOOD IMMUNIZATION RATES BY ETHNICITY, 1994, 1997

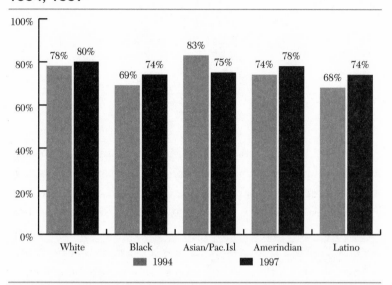

Source: Centers for Disease Control, National Immunization Survey, 1998

compared to whites and Asians. Even though the trend is upward for all racial groups, in 1997 blacks were being immunized at the rates at which whites were during the early 1990s. Easily controlled diseases such as rubella and pertussis become problems as black boys enter their autumn years. Linked with inconsistent health care at early ages are the myths concerning violence among black males. Drugs and alcohol are usually involved with violent crime, and the widely held perception is that adolescent black males use these substances as psychological "oil" in order to commit the crimes. In fact, drugs are used at much higher rates primarily among *whites* in the commitment of crime, as shown in Chart 9.

The drugged-out, hulking, gun-toting black adolescent in a dark hood and baggy pants and looking for violence is a myth.

CHART 9: DRUG OR ALCOHOL USE BY OFFENDER

Race of Victim	Total	Alcohol	Drugs
White	100%	29%	8%
Black	100%	21%	7%
Asian	100%	20%	3%

Source: Bureau of Justice Statistics, *American Indians and Crime*, February 1999

The fact remains, however, that black boys in the autumn of their lives die faster and more frequently than other boys. I believe this is due, in part, to the absence of rites-of-passage ceremonies for black boys. The Native American vision quest, the Jewish bar mitzvah, and even adolescent baptism in more fundamental Christian churches are all rites of passages that celebrate a boy's journey into manhood; as such, these ceremonies have major impact on them. Rocano Gilbert and Cheo Taylor's *Simba*—Kiswahili for "lion"—program, which was established during the 1990s, has provided rites-of-passage ceremonies to dozens of boys in California. According to Taylor, they have had a profound change on the boys and their community: "Violence, crime, poverty, drug abuse and murder can be totally eliminated by people making different choices. These choices are made as a result of how individuals see themselves and others, and how they think, feel and act towards themselves and others."

Autumn Warriors Councils

While throughout their lives black boys are at risk for having health problems, being victims of homicide, and being under-taught by schools, their teenage years are, paradoxically, a time of danger and a time of opportunity. There is an obsession among social scientists for detailing the challenges of black male adolescents while providing few remedies for overcoming these problems. Of course they have a high rate of fratricidal homicide; of course their educational issues need elaboration; we already know most of this. This is a critical period for black boys; it is the stage when options for changing self-destructive behavior are fewer and paths to social extinction wider. The Young Warriors Councils need to be even more vigilant in making sure these years are successfully negotiated.

The Warriors Councils should prepare for a rites-of-passage week when Young Warriors reach the age of thirteen; this ceremony should be attended by the council members who have been involved with the boys for thirteen years. The oldest member of the Warriors Council should direct the rite-of-passage ceremony. That young black men understand how elder black men have dealt with racism and other obstacles in their lives is important; therefore, the ceremony should include a one-hour videotaped interview with an elder male in the community who is at least seventy years old.

At the end of the week, the boy conducting the interview should present the videotape to the council. During this same week, the *elder* should interview the *initiate*. These two interviews serve a dual purpose: to gather information and to bond the boy to his past and his future. The elder black male becomes a true "role model" for the boy and teaches him his obligations to the African-American community. A study done by Dr. Raymond Coward of the National Institute on Aging revealed that older blacks are twice as likely to receive total care by family members than older whites. By listening to their elders recite "how they got over," young boys need to understand that "care" is more than medical care. The interviews also give the elder an opportunity to reconnect with his past, renew his sense of self-esteem, and continue his contributions to the future of his community.

Rites-of-passage ceremonies vary greatly from city to city and community to community, similar to the way Poro Societies vary in West Africa. I have participated in a variety of these ceremonies around the country, and I am excited by the creativity of those involved. The type of ceremony is not as important as the encouragement to Cinque's sons to continue a tradition that began centuries ago but was all but lost during the period of enslavement. That the ceremonies incorporate the same African-centered values found in the ancestral homeland of black Americans is important. Rites-of-passage ceremonies provide social support for African-American males, much like the psychological and social support that helped them survive the *Amistad* and free themselves to return home. All rites-of-passage ceremonies should contain the following:

1. Two rites-of-passage ceremonies should be conducted during the year for the seven Young Warriors. For boys born between January 1 and June 30, a ceremony should be conducted on or before July 1. For the Young Warriors whose birthdays fall between July 1 and December 31, a second ceremony should be conducted on the first night of Kwanzaa (*Umoja*). Invitations for the two ceremonies should go to members of the boys' immediate family, other relatives, and friends.

2. The oldest man and oldest woman in the Young Warriors Council should perform the pouring of libations. The libation ceremony should honor the boy's thirteen-year involvement with both the Birthing Circle and the Warriors Council, and

should honor the ancestors and link the young man with his ancestral ties to Africa. For example, the elders could pour water on a plant in front of the gathering. A sample libation recitation that can be shared by the elder man and woman during this part of the ritual follows:

> Ancestors, we know that you are honored by [name of Young Warrior] being here today. [Pour part of the water into the plant.] He has been with us for thirteen years, and honored the sacrifices that all of you made while you were on earth. [Pour more of the water into the plant.] [Name of Young Warrior] has the spirit of Malcolm X, the patience of Joseph Cinque, the strength of Martin Delaney, and the kindness of his father [substitute names as appropriate for the boy, and pour a third portion of the water.] We know that you will be with [name of Young Warrior] as he begins his journey into manhood. We know that he will be strong, wise, and kind to his family, to women, to children, to other brothers, and to himself. [Pour remaining water.]

Libation recitation can take many forms, but keeping the boy and the ancestors central to the ceremony should be paramount.

3. The boy's immediate family should make three brief testimonies. This can be done by the parents, guardians, and/or siblings of the boy and should take no more than ten minutes. The testimonies should praise the boy, recite humorous anecdotes, and provide proof to the gathering that the boy has been mature and deserves to be called a man.

4. An elder woman should then read a passage (no more than five minutes) from a black writer that has been meaningful to the boy during his life. The elder woman should explain why she chose the passage, then read the poem prose that is symbolic of the initiate's life.

5. Similar to the previous reading, the boy should read a passage that is meaningful to him. It, too, should be no more than ten minutes and carefully chosen.

6. Following this, the gathering should watch the video interview. It should be shown without comment; if done well, it will convey the importance of older black men mentoring younger ones. A brief discussion should follow, with the initiate and the elder man answering questions from the audience.

7. As the final act of the ceremony, the same elder man and woman who opened the ceremony should give to the boys a larger piece of *Kente* cloth. This should be followed with gifts to the new man and a *karamu*, in which all participate.

Remember, this is a *suggested* rites-of-passage ceremony. It is provided as an example; the creativity of the Young Warriors Councils can embrace a variety of rituals conducive to inducting the boys into manhood. After the ceremony is complete, it is paramount that the councils continue their once-per-month meetings and maintain support for the boys as they enter full adulthood.

How should this be done? Like Poro Society, if the Warriors Councils have been taught correctly, the young men will have a set of values based on the Four Cs. They will have a broad understanding of their obligation to family, community, and themselves that will equip them, as Cinque was equipped, to cope with an assortment of social, legal, and educational circumstances. But the Warriors Councils must reinforce these values until the young man is twenty-one. Initially, this should occur in the monthly meetings, but gradually, over a period of two years, the young men themselves must continue their association with one another, much as Cinque relied on the Mende men captured on the *Amistad* to secure freedom for all fifty-two captives. According to court documents and eyewitness accounts, the Poro Society that the Mende captives of the *Amistad* belonged to persisted during their Connecticut imprisonment. They consulted with and made suggestions to one another, appointed Cinque as their primary spokesperson, and passed along to one another information that would shed light on their captivity. The Warriors Councils should promote comparable conduct among the new initiates. Members of the council will find that the Young Warriors naturally appoint leaders among themselves for certain tasks and responsibilities. The young men should never be encouraged to model themselves after "Black Greek letter" fraternities that often haze their new members and have values only tangentially related to African-centered values.

The cohesiveness among the Young Warriors will be severely tested if one of them "gets into trouble." Trouble can occur if one of them is arrested or detained for things he did not do. The legal preparation they received during their summer years will be tested during such periods. The adults in the council should have names of attorneys, physicians, and other persons readily available when legal crises arise. The council should act on behalf of the young man for events that he is too young to handle. At all times each member of the council should carry the phone numbers of all the other members so that they can reach one another quickly. This is very important; adolescent black boys are often coerced into confessions by law enforcement agents. On several occasions, I have seen young black men sitting in parking lots, handcuffed, with several police cars surrounding them. Officers yelling and headlights glaring in their faces make for a horrendous scene, with the terrified youngsters looking bewildered and afraid. While I am sure that the heavy-handed tactics used by police can sometimes be justified, I am equally sure that in many cases they are not. Police brutality and harsh sentencing are real and are directed disproportionately toward young black males. In 2000, 50 percent of juveniles on Death Row were black. Young Warriors Councils should be aware of such data and do whatever they can to help their members avoid contact with the criminal justice system, as well as help those who do come in contact with law enforcement.

Educational Issues

The investment club should have grown substantially by now, with an eye toward ensuring that each of the seven Young Warriors is looking toward education beyond high school. Time should be set aside in the regular monthly meetings to discuss both current and future educational issues affecting the boys' lives. Continued exposure to black male role models should reinforce the idea that formal education is of paramount importance to Young Warriors.

During the eleventh grade, tours of historically black colleges and universities should be planned, and the testing and application procedure should be guided by an adult member of the council. The boys should schedule time with their high school guidance counselors; council members must monitor these sessions since black boys' aspirations are often detoured in these offices. I have asked dozens of *teachers* about their own "guidance" during this period, and many have reported hearing discouraging words from insensitive counselors about higher education. At Fisk, students have reported to me how white counselors discouraged them from attending a historically black university in favor of a local community college. Counselors may ask disparaging questions about the "quality" of education students may receive, despite the fact that historically black universities have produced W.E.B. Du Bois, Nikki Giovanni, Martin Luther King, Toni Morrison, and so many more. The councils should act as a watchdog over such bad advice and, as during the other seasons, intervene if necessary.

Work

All Young Warriors should be encouraged to work after school when they turn sixteen. Part-time work outside the home teaches discipline and increases children's economic responsibility. A portion of the Young Warriors' pay should be set aside for the investment fund. However, working outside the home should never interfere with the boys' education. In this sense, all extracurricular activities, including work, should be subjugated to the boy doing well in middle and high school. The boys should integrate the principle of *Ujima* (collective work and responsibility) into how they conduct themselves in whatever work they do. Work should be valued as a learning experience, even if it involves flipping hamburgers or ushering at a sporting event. Elders should teach how the value of work is linked to the community and how money can contribute to uplifting persons

within it. Respecting places where people work is also important. When I was a child, my mother once told me that we
should be careful about littering in public buildings because
"nine times out of ten, one of ours is cleaning it up at night."
This axiom stuck with me throughout my life, and it was an early
lesson in respecting the work of others.

Black Men and Women

At each stage, the Young Warriors Councils discuss the primacy
of the relationship between black men and women. All of the rituals involved in bringing the boy to manhood show the importance of black males learning to respect black females. Poro
Society consistently taught its initiates the importance of
respecting women and deemphasized sexist attitudes toward
girls and women. The autumn Warriors Councils should focus
some of their activities on frank and open discussions about sexuality and its role in the healthy development of black couples.
In particular, council members should invite counselors and
physicians to join discussion groups. Often adolescents distort
information about sex regardless of race. Autumn may be the
last time this information is shaped in a positive way for the boys.

Warriors Councils should conduct lengthy discussions on the
history of black male and female relationships during this
period. Familial relationships among Africans in America were
damaged by enslavement's legacy, and still linger despite denials
by White Way parents. Randall Robinson's book *The Debt: What
America Owes to Blacks* shows how white privilege's bitter fruits
were nurtured by the roots of slavery sunk deep into the barren
soil of American racism. He makes the all-too-often-ignored
connections between contemporary American institutions and

their embarrassing connections to slavery. Aetna Life, the largest life insurance company in America, for example, insured the lives of slaves from its beginnings in 1853. Slave owners took out policies on their slaves and received death benefits when they died. Nothing, of course, was given to the deceased's immediate family. In 2000, Aetna "apologized" for this history and its CEO referred to it as a "deplorable practice." Young Warriors during their autumn years should learn this history; those who encourage people to "forget about it and move on" should be viewed with suspicion.

Since the success of Terry McMillan's *Waiting to Exhale*, young people have read a spate of black romance novels with the fairly common theme of almost irreconcilable problems between black men and black women. Even before these books, Michele Wallace's 1979 best-seller, *Black Macho and the Myth of the Superwoman*, was dubiously touted by *Ms.* magazine as one of the most important treatises ever written by a black woman. In *Black Macho*, Wallace analyzes from a feminist perspective the sexual dynamic of the transition from civil rights to black liberation. This is what she found: "There is a profound distrust, even hatred between black men and black women. It has been nursed along not only by racism on the part of whites but also by an almost deliberate ignorance on the part of blacks about the sexual politics of their experience in this country."

Hatred between black men and black women? In some cases, yes. But in most cases, no. Persons who couldn't care less about our relationships often do focus on the problems between black men and black women. White feminists proclaimed *Black Macho* to be a frank discussion about the relationships between blacks, as if such a discussion were really important to the white feminist movement.

Moreover, films and books during the 1980s created heated

discussions on this incendiary topic. *The Women of Brewster Place* and *The Color Purple* were both met with ridicule and scorn by insecure black men who saw Gloria Naylor and Alice Walker as "betrayers of black manhood." In fact, these books and films merely scratched the surface of deeper problems that have existed for centuries between black men and black women under white supremacy. These books drew attention to the inherent sexism during the civil rights period when freedom for African Americans was somehow associated with men and not women. "Prone," the infamous answer by a civil rights worker about where the best "place" for women was during the 1960s, had been challenged by Ella Baker and other women. They found new energy with Angela Davis, Alice Walker, and bell hooks, who gave renewed meaning to Sojourner Truth's words that "among the blacks there are women and among the women there are blacks."

But rarely were substantive dialogues between black men and black women held regarding the wedges that had been deliberately driven between them by racism. More radical theorists, such as Haki Madhubuti and Neely Fuller, saw this as the essential problem between us. However, it is tempting to focus on the more obvious results of racism's *impact* on these relationships than on the actual *source*. After all, conservatives say "white supremacy" is a slippery, vague, and nebulous concept, similar to Melville's great white whale. They argue rather weakly that it remains elusive and becomes even more so when it is attached to contemporary relationships between black men and black women.

It was easy to see how such disruptions occurred during our period of enslavement, with the rape of black women, their sale by the masters, and the controlled sexual access that black women and black men had with one another on plantations. It is much harder to see how, 150 years later, the residual effects of slavery would haunt our relationships, even though Toni Morrison writes about it in *Beloved*, and Alice Walker in *The Color Purple*. Black men and black women, through the ingenious nexus of Hollywood and the media, would eventually blame each other for the difficulties between them, leaving racism out of these discussions. It is worth repeating Ayi Kwei Armah's view, in his book *Two Thousand Seasons*, of how our relationships were the focus of white supremacy:

> *There is no beauty but in the relationships.*
> *Nothing cut off by itself is beautiful.*
> *Never can things in destructive relationships be beautiful.*
> *All beauty is in the creative purpose of our relationships;*
> *All ugliness is in the destructive aims of the destroyer's*
>   *arrangements.*

Armah believes, as do I, that the primary attack, which dislocated black men and black women from Africa and one another, was deliberate and was expressed in many ways. The inability of black men and black women to protect one another during enslavement produced feelings of impotence and helplessness on both sides. Neither could protect their children from being slaughtered, beaten, or sold. The reality behind the poignant portrayal of Kizzy being sold in *Roots* was the greatest threat to the parents of any enslaved child. The last narratives spoken by enslaved African Americans during the 1930s on their enslavement indicated a morbid fear of being sold that was often used to coerce them into subjection.

Nothing changed during the Jim Crow era, when nearly

every day black men and black women were lynched somewhere in the United States. Accounts of these lynchings horrify the readers and question the humanity of the perpetrators. Cobb cites a case recorded in the *Vicksburg Evening-Post* during the 1920s in which a black Mississippi couple was lynched for allegedly killing a white man:

> The blacks were forced to hold out their hands while one finger at a time was chopped off. The fingers were distributed as souvenirs. The ears of the murders [*sic*] were cut off. Hobert was beaten severely, his skull was fractured, and one of his eyes, knocked with a stick, hung by a shred from the socket. . . . [A] large corkscrew . . . was bored into the man and woman . . . and then pulled out, the spirals tearing out big pieces of raw, quivering flesh. Then the crowd burned them at the stake, after partially filling their mouths and nostrils with mud to prevent a fast death from smoke inhalation.

The lynching of Mary Turner, reported in *The Crisis* in 1918, confirms the inability of black men and black women to protect one another from violence. After her husband had been lynched in Valdosta, Georgia, Turner made the mistake of making public her intention of seeing her husband's murderers put to death. When word of her defiant promise reached those who had participated in her husband's murder, they kidnapped her from her house. Although she was eight months pregnant, she was hanged upside down from a tree and bathed with gasoline. After burning her clothes from her body, her stomach was cut open and the infant fell to the ground. It gave out a whimper before a man crushed the baby's head with his shoe. When found, Ms.

Turner's body was riddled with hundreds of bullets. Her murder was casually reported by the press as the result of her "unwise remarks" concerning her husband's death.

Throughout the civil rights era the violence directed toward black men and black women continued with the notorious killing of Emmett Till, the arrest of Rosa Parks, the beating of Fannie Lou Hamer, and the assassination of Martin Luther King Jr., to name only a few. We often forget how both men and women were affected by this violence. Emmett Till's mother told the Chicago funeral directors to leave her son's coffin open so that people could see the horrors done to her son. In 1955, she had sent her son to Money, Mississippi, to visit relatives; the fourteen-year-old Till on a dare flirted with a white female store clerk named Carolyn Bryant. A few days later, Bryant's husband, Roy, and J. W. Milam abducted Till from his uncle's house. His body was found three days later, beaten beyond recognition, an eye gouged out, and a bullet in his skull, which had apparently been crushed with an ax. Till was found in the Tallahatchie River, weighed down with a 150-pound cotton-gin fan. Blacks were terrified, and it was simply unthinkable for one to testify against a white man accused of a racial crime. However, Emmett's sixty-four-year-old uncle, Mose Wright, defied custom; at risk to his life, he agreed to be a witness at the trial of the two men accused of killing Emmett. When the prosecutor asked Wright to identify the men who had abducted his nephew, he stood up, pointed to Milam and Bryant, and said, "Dar he."

In the end, however, Wright's incredible courage made no difference. Milam and Bryant's attorney told the all-white, all-male jury in his closing statement, "Your fathers will turn over in their graves if [they are found guilty], and I'm sure that every last Anglo-Saxon one of you has the courage to free these men in the face of that [outside] pressure." The jurors listened to him, deliberated for about an hour, then returned a "not guilty" verdict. The foreman later said, "I feel the state failed to prove the identity of the body." I remember as a child being afraid to go to sleep after looking at the gruesome photo of Till displayed on the cover of *Jet* magazine.

In our mind's eye, we also see the famous funeral photo of Coretta Scott King and her children, and we realize the enormous impact that racism has on the relationships of black men and black women. The women in James Byrd Jr.'s life suffered after his lynching in Jasper, Texas. His decapitated body, after being dragged by three white men on a lonely Texas road, was the crime he paid for being a black man at the wrong place at the wrong time. Dr. Thomas Brown, the pathologist who testified at Byrd's murderers' trial in 1999, described the victim's last moments in his testimony, which was quoted by the Associated Press and Reuters:

> Brown said the 49-year-old Byrd was still alive as he bounced down the road June 7, breaking most of his ribs, shredding his knees and his elbows, fracturing bone and tearing cartilage. Brown said Byrd struggled with his torso to keep his head off the road, and in the process was castrated.
>
> The pathologist said Byrd was probably conscious until he grew so weary that his body flipped off the road and into a concrete culvert, about halfway through his three-mile ordeal, when his 'head, shoulder and right arm were separated.'
>
> Prosecutor Pat Hardy described those last moments: "The gentleman was alive and was alive up until the time he pretty much exploded when he hit the culvert. And you

can imagine the pain he went through from the injuries he had."

His aunts, sisters, and mother shared in the horror of his death at the hands of murderous white males, who have in the past haunted and continue to haunt our relationships. We often forget how the horrors of racism affect black men *and* black women, and mediate our relationships in a variety of ways.

This is a sordid but necessary history for Young Warriors to learn during the autumn of their lives. Taught correctly, these stories will instill within them a sense of how they can either contribute to this history or teach others how the sacred bond between black men and black women should be preserved. Elders in the councils should teach that it is not by accident that images presented to young black people are part of a long history of destroying the sacred bonds between black men and women stolen from Africa.

Conclusion

Despite the role of discipline in the autumn Warriors Councils, these groups should not be viewed as militaristic or rigid. Monitoring young men's progress does not mean that there is no room to attend sporting activities, proms, field trips, and other activities of a typical teenage boy. The councils play a stabilizing role in the boys' lives and become an extended family that they can rely on. Each boy is simply surrounded by a true "village" that helps him learn what being a man is all about. The autumn years are important for this lesson; it is the last period when the boy is dependent on adult supervision. These lessons need to be learned well as the young man enters the winter of his life.

7

The Seasons of Our Sons: Winter, Ages 22 Through Homegoing

> *For you are father to the orphan, husband to the widow, brother to the rejected woman, apron to the motherless.* —KHUN ANUP, 1650 B.C.

Harold

His oldest son was in jail, and he had just suffered his second heart attack. Bills were left unopened on the kitchen table because there was no money to pay them. His two youngest sons were in school and needed financial support. His pride eventually yielded but prevented him for many years to allow his wife to work; he adhered to the strictest of Eurocentric beliefs that only he could be the "breadwinner." His two daughters were out on their own, the oldest married to a churchgoing southern man who loved her dearly, the younger one in and out of an abusive relationship with a man who would eventually die of a heart attack before reaching forty.

Since this was during the pre-bypass era, it was impossible to do anything about Harold's heart. It beat as best it could and was fed nitroglycerin when it didn't do that very well. Shredded wheat, skim milk, and other healthy foods had nearly replaced

THE WARRIOR METHOD   179

the unhealthy diet that he, like most African-American men, indulged in. Harold tried hard to stick to the healthy regime so that he might eke out a few more beats and thus a few more years with his family.

I saw him during this period angry, abusive toward his wife, sullen about having to work so hard and only able to do it, and depressed because he was uninsurable due to his heart condition. When Harold purchased his first house at the age of fifty-one, it was more stimulating, at least psychologically, than the defibrillator that had been used to restart his heart on several occasions. He also bought his first car a year later—a Deuce and a Quarter—that was as long as the living room in the new bungalow that meant so much to him and Dorothy. They began to travel widely, to places like Pittsburgh, Toronto, and Chicago, in the silver-and-black Buick. He helped his oldest son find a good job despite his prison record. Even though Harold had not gone to college, he was adamant that his two younger sons would, and he helped them to do so with both emotional and financial support. He dispensed wisdom that would stay with his children long after he'd gone from their lives. "If you make your bed hard, you've got to lie on it" and "He who knows and knows he knows is wise, follow him" were two of his favorite quotes.

Like most older black men—older being any who survive the age of fifty—Harold was focused on making sure that there would be a legacy to pass on to his children and his grandchildren. He knew the mistake he had made in waiting to buy a house, treating his wife violently, and simply working too hard when he should have taken it easy. During Thanksgiving gatherings, Christmas celebrations, and family reunions, he began to teach his children from his own experiences. He would speak to them, usually one-on-one, as if he did not want to risk the possibility that someone would challenge him. His sons and daughters would relate what he said privately to one another and swap the information among themselves. They had forgiven him of his past wrongs and were understanding of things that were happening to him physically and emotionally at this time in his life.

At sixty-four Harold died of a stroke as he sat waiting to take Dorothy to work. Quietly humming to himself, a blood vessel popped in his head; he breathed his last breath, then slumped over in his favorite chair. Dorothy walked into the living room, saw him in the chair, and began to cry. She would follow him with lung cancer just four years later, and my brother Ron and I would choose the spot in the cemetery where they would rest together with the ancestors.

Like so many other black men, my father knew that life was lived in a world of white supremacy. He railed against it from as far back as I could remember, and he always told us to do the same. It was frustrating to see how the white world punished him for standing up against discrimination in the steel mills of Pittsburgh and the unions of Cleveland.

He had been living in Pittsburgh when Josh Gibson played with the Homestead Grays in the Negro Baseball Leagues, and he was an avid baseball fan. He bragged about the fact that Babe Ruth, that American icon, couldn't hold a candle to Josh Gibson's power at home plate. I realize now that baseball was to black men during the Depression what basketball is for young black men today. They lived it, talked about it, and were proud of Jackie Robinson's resilience against racism. Dad was a good ballplayer in his own right, and he taught his sons the game, as well as how to keep meticulous box scores for all of the players, especially the 1950s black players, such as Lary Doby and Minnie Minoso.

He knew that he had often treated my mother badly, and he tried to make up for it as he grew older. Part of the obligation of being a black man during his winter months is to tell others what they need to know about navigating the waters of racism in school, work, and social situations. My father did this as best he could with the tools he had, while supporting his family during a period when doing all of this was very hard. His children saw this and understood it.

We Are the Men Our Ancestors Prayed For

My father resisted. Sometimes he was successful, sometimes he wasn't. Our generation of black men no longer has to succumb to physical and psychological control the way our ancestors had to during their enslavement. We have choices. To be sure, these choices still occur with a backdrop of racism, but we have them and can exercise them effectively when we factor in how racism mediates these choices. We can enter the courts to seek redress for wrongs against us. Like Cinque, we can let people know that even though they view us as only recent members of the human race, we come from a long line of strong men, and will continue to be so for centuries to come. We always understood the importance of letting others know we had brains, we just didn't have the wherewithal to show it. So even though we know our sons have only a 1 in 52,000 chance of being a player in the National Basketball Association, we still encourage playing the sport for the sense of teamwork and dedication it inspires.

We can no longer act as conduits for drugs in our communities or sell our souls to Hollywood studios and record company executives, just for meager monetary gain and the sanction to demean our brothers and sisters. We fail at capitalizing on our popularity like Ronald Reagan, G. Gordon Liddy, Oliver North, and Bill Bradley, and so we are left wondering what a Michael Jordan, Bill Cosby, or Kareem Abdul-Jabbar might do as a senator or president. We agonize to a man when we see our brothers shooting each other, and we rejoice with them as a Mandela and a Tutu tell the world what time it is.

Winter starts at twenty-two in the lives of black men. This is a dangerous time for us, the period when we direct the greatest homicidal violence toward one another. The only way to counter or prevent this violence is early intervention—Birthing Circles, Young Warriors Councils, the Four Cs—which will heighten self-esteem, self-awareness, and, subsequently, lower the number of homicidal deaths among young black men.

Role Models

Black men, for they are now indeed men, should begin to tell their peers what being a man means to them. Black boys who become men and shun drugs, violence, and predatory behavior toward their community should all be viewed as role models rather than those who have finished college, or have become "successful" businessmen. "Role model" is a much misunderstood term and has become increasingly meaningless when used in terms of aiding the African-American community to achieve certain goals. A noble concept, it is oversold as a way to help black boys in trouble. In many cases the idea is a way of opting out of doing the hard and necessary interventions that would truly change the boys' lives for the better.

Like other black professional men, I have been asked on numerous occasions to be a "role model" for young black boys and girls by doing volunteer work and by simply being around them. My ambivalence about this designation lies not so much in

my feelings that such volunteer work is useless, but that it limits
the definition of "role model" to black professional men.

Recently I was asked to participate in such a session honoring
a "leader" of a midsize city in the South. He was rich, powerful,
drove a luxury car, and lived in an all-white neighborhood. Based
on these acquisitions, he was considered "successful." I had little
respect for the brother, who was being touted as a "role model,"
because he had done numerous things to harm black people in
the city. He smiled as he received the award, and I thought
about the numerous people he had professionally assassinated at
the behest of his white benefactors. He now epitomized the
notion of a Super Slave as his white sponsors told the wide-eyed
boys sitting before him how he was a "role model" for them. In
older times he would be considered a "credit to his race"—now
he was simply a puppet of color for whites, and was used as a disruptive force in the local African-American community.

It is difficult for black men to sanction men like these publicly since it bruises egos and creates divisions within our communities. A recent public criticism of Vernon Jordan by Randall
Robinson brought scathing rebukes by several black journalists
who saw Jordan as a power broker who deserved respect and
deference. Critiques of African-American communities by so-
called neo-conservatives are often applauded and blessed by
whites. Publicly denouncing our "role models" as sellouts to the
needs of all black people is dismissed as the ravings of marginal-
ized radicals. I have watched such nationally known black "leaders" in various arenas proclaim their disdain for Louis Farrakhan,
Kweisi Mfume, or Al Sharpton to the overwhelming praise of
their powerful white supporters. Black men must be careful that
the role models they become are not mere cardboard carica-
tures of white persons who ultimately do not want the best for
African Americans. Furthermore, they must measure the worth

of any leader by deeds, not words, and they must choose carefully whom they repudiate or praise so as not to be manipulated
by whites who feel threatened by independent black men and
the power they wield.

What Can Black Men and Women Learn About Each Other?

African Americans are taught to eat generously from the boun-
ties of white supremacist culture but only nibble at knowledge
about themselves. The old saying in African-American communities that the "white man's ice is colder than the black man's"
reflects another rumor of inferiority that somehow "theirs" is
better than "ours."

It is the same with black men's and black women's knowledge
of one another. I have given workshops on black relationships in
which I ask how many black men and black women there are in
the United States. The range of answers has not to do so much
with educational levels or cultural intelligence as it does with the
lack of accurate information about black men and black women
beyond popular media. There are simply too few books available
for us to know hard-core facts about each other. We often enter
heated discussions about our relationships based more on fiction
than fact. The appalling lack of hard information shared
between us determines many of the ways we interact toward one
another, and creates misunderstandings and faulty generalizations about what we mean to each other.

One piece of information that enlightens our relationships is
the *sex ratio*, which is defined as the number of men per one
hundred women in a selected population. When just these data
are presented to workshops of black men and black women, a

lightbulb seems to go on in the room. Chart 10 illustrates the sex ratio since 1920 for whites and blacks in the United States, the implications of which are enormous. Slightly over 1.8 million black women in the United States have no men of marriageable age available for them. These figures do not include black men who are gay, confirmed bachelors, in relationships with nonblack women, or are incarcerated. Adding these to the total number of "unavailable" black men could increase the figure to 2.5 million.

This discussion should not be construed to imply that black women *need* a black man in their lives. Indeed, there are black women who are lesbian, single by choice, committed to white men, or in prison. What is important is that black women have fewer choices than their white counterparts when it comes to the availability of men.

Many books and magazines feature articles about these numbers. Some black men even take perverse advantage of it. Often black women get angry about it. I have heard black women say, "Men are a luxury" and "I don't need a man in my life." This may or may not be true, and in some case Cinque's sons reinforce

CHART 10: UNITED STATES SEX RATIO BY RACE: 1920–1990

Year	Whites	Blacks
1920	104.4	99.2
1930	102.9	97.0
1940	101.2	95.0
1950	99.0	93.7
1960	97.4	93.3
1970	95.3	90.8
1980	94.8	89.6
1990	95.9	89.8

these ideas by their actions toward women. I have heard black men brag about the fact that their choices of women are vast because they are "in demand." My megalomaniacal brothers who say such things have no anchoring in African traditions that seek balance rather than power in their male-female relationships. They are psychologically immature when it comes to conducting healthy relationships with women, and they see women as things to be manipulated rather than persons to be cherished.

The bitterness that many black women feel toward black men in many cases is well founded. Brothers can do better but often don't. They rationalize their misogyny in rap lyrics that degrade black women. Claiming that this is what "the Sisters want to hear" and referring to women as female dogs strengthens the alienation between them. Moreover, viewing a black woman as "a bitch" puts her even lower than the "dawg" black men "affectionately" call one another.

At a recent speaking engagement at a historically black college, several young black men just entering the winter years of their life defended their use of the terms "bitch," "dawg," and "nigga," despite very vocal protestations from the women in the audience. The men were firm in their belief that these terms were endearing and showed affection for themselves and "their women." Only a handful of black men in the audience objected to their use, and these men were derided for being "punks." One woman in the audience looked pleadingly at me and said that this is why there are so many problems between black men and black women—because we are not listening to each other. Her words rang true, and I asked her what could be done to improve the communication. She said that we simply don't listen to one another, that we already have our minds made up about where the other is coming from. I agreed.

As the new millennium begins, there is little listening and

even less communicating between black men and black women. Perhaps the sheer gap in numbers forces us to talk about and not listen to one another. One female told me during a Kwanzaa celebration, "Sisters don't have enough black men to 'practice' on in the most basic interactions." I asked her what she meant, and she said that black women have to imagine what black men feel, think, and do because there simply aren't enough to demonstrate what being a black man is all about. She went on and compared learning about black men with learning to swim: you can read all the books in the world about it, but you really won't learn anything unless you jump in the water. Her metaphor ended with her comment that there was no pool, no water, and no bathing suits for many women who simply want to know things about black men. "We are left to guess what black men want, feel, think, and know, and we simply have no place to practice these things."

A deliberate psychological education must begin if black men and black women are to get to know one another. A few years ago a female friend and I began running groups called Seminars on African-American Relationships (SOAR), in which for two hours once a week black men and black women simply talked to one another about themselves and the things important to them. The fifteen to twenty members, half men and half women, expressed their delight in meeting and just talking. After a month, however, we noticed that a few black men were beginning to fall by the wayside. I called several of them, and they reported that some of the things being said in the group were hitting "too close to home" and that they were feeling uncomfortable. I encouraged them to come back and talk to the group about their experience, though I knew it wasn't going to happen. Not wanting the group to become disproportionate by gender, I told the remaining members how the Brothers felt. Surprisingly,

both men and women said that these were simply excuses for
miscommunication or for no communication. They believed that
the men who left would leave anyway and opt for "safer" com-
munications, which in their case meant no communication at all.
The remaining members wanted to continue, despite the three-
to-one ratio that had resulted from members dropping out. I was
not sure that the group should dismiss the men who'd stopped
coming so easily. Should they be coaxed into returning to share
their feelings? I think that black men are taught at young ages to
hide, suppress, and otherwise ignore the part of them that may
be considered tender. One might argue that this has nothing to
do with color, since all men are emotionally inhibited. All men
are, but black men have inherited a social climate where speaking one's thoughts can actually be dangerous. My father, similar
to other black fathers, taught us what to say when confronted by
white police officers. We were also taught how to talk to white
bosses and how to avoid making white males feel threatened by
our presence. Most white males receive a surplus of confidence
builders in social situations since their environments affirm their
white maleness. Not so with black men. The machismo taught to
black boys beginning at early ages sometimes works to keep
them insulated against racism, but it discourages expressions of
love, hurt, and pain. It leaves black women feeling alone in con-
versations with us; the communication is often a one-way effort,
met on occasion with a grunt from black men. In group situations with other black men, bullshitting replaces true expressions of feelings. If a brother does gather the courage to speak of
his vulnerability with another black man, he can be faced with
ridicule or dismissed as a punk.

I have observed black filmgoers, both male and female, laugh
at black films such as *Fresh, The Hurricane,* and *Beloved,* that
are emotionally painful to watch. The laughter is a defense

against seeing our own condition placed on the wide screen and being unable to connect with the helpless feelings that are uncovered. Black men are particularly prone to dismissing feelings that make them less "hard" in a world that requires hardness for survival.

Black boys, who often hear the older women in their lives make negative comments about black men, are subject to this early push toward emotional isolation. The lover who ran out on her, the father she never saw, the brother who is unwilling or unable to help financially—are all bogeymen projected onto her impressionable young son. Black men must be bad because Mom says they are bad, the boy reasons; without contrary evidence, these phrases become mantras boys repeat to themselves and other black boys. They grow up with ideas about manhood that are heavily influenced by women who may be bitter about men. Joined by some brothers who are simply trifling, young black males become the tangible results of self-fulfilling prophecies. This vicious cycle will continue unless very early intervention takes place.

Healthy Black Relationships: Beloved in Our Lives

The inability of black men and black women to sustain relationships unmediated by race has been nearly total since they were first captured in Africa. This topic, if discussed, would create greater cohesiveness in our relationships. Morrison's ghostly child-woman Beloved, in her book by the same name, represents how the relationships between black men and women are haunted by the unresolved racism that has damaged them. Sethe's poignant words about her rapists, "They took my milk," are still relevant to what black women face today. They should discuss this connection with the men in their lives. Likewise, black men feel a connection with Halle, whose insanity was triggered by watching the rape of his wife and being unable to stop it. It is important for black men in the winter of their lives to share this connection they feel with their women. To suppose that Beloved's ghost no longer haunts the lives of black people in America, and indeed the world, is delusional. She is the fruit of the horrors we sustain as we try to establish families for our children and ourselves. The chokeberry tree on Sethe's back, kissed by Paul D, is a reminder of how black men and women should seek to heal the wounds inflicted on us by a culture determined to sever bonds between us.

Black men in search of the woman who will be "the one" in their lives should take heed of Sixo, Paul D's friend at Sweet Home, who walked twenty-eight miles once a week to be with his "Thirty-Mile Woman" for one hour. His description of what he wants in a woman is one of the most sublime in black literature:

> Paul D. sits down in the rocking chair, and examines the quilt patched in carnival colors. His hands are limp between his knees. There are too many things to feel about this woman. His head hurts. Suddenly he remembers Sixo trying to describe what he felt about the Thirty-Mile Woman. "She is a friend of my mind. She gathers me, man. The pieces I am, she gathers them and give them back to me in all the right order. It's good, you know, when you got a woman who is a friend of your mind."

"A friend of your mind." Morrison's words are as important to women as they are to men. I have seen in my work black women who knowingly opt for men and women who are not friends of their mind. They do not effect the healing described in *Beloved*; instead they are wandering hopelessly in relationships that are meaningless, attributable to black men being "just dogs" and black women who are "just bitches." This is a simple conclusion to a problem that we rarely discuss among ourselves at functional levels. A female friend of mine recently said that she would not discuss her problems with white people or with black men. Moreover, she told me that many of her black female friends were simply dysfunctional when it came to black male/female relationships. My friend is living with a lot of pain, confusion, and anger, but she has no communication with black men who are the source of much of her anger. Ultimately, these situations all too often translate into negative comments made about black men in front of black boys in the spring and summer months of their lives. They hear too often that black men "ain't shit," and they begin to harbor the anger that eventually translates into the poisonous hate-filled lyrics of unconscious rappers paid handsomely by record executives to ignite further misogynistic behavior among black boys and men. It is a vicious cycle.

In the end, Beloved disappears, after Sethe confronts her demons and the black women of Cincinnati provide her with spiritual support for her unresolved pain. What is important, however, is that her exorcism is incomplete until Paul D returns to her life and tells her, "You your best thing." Sethe is unbelieving until she answers her question, "Me? Me?" Only when he answers yes can they begin their long journey to reconciliation and understanding. It is the same for us today.

8

A Summary of the Seasons

Historians have speculated for years about the *Amistad* incident and its leader, Sengbeh Pieh. Few people in African-American history have had the impact on the treatment of Africans in America more than Pieh. What motivated him to rebel against his enslavement and direct his captors to take him back to his homeland of Sierra Leone? How could he effect such a successful rebellion with a handful of men and women on a voyage that his buyers saw as a relatively routine "shopping trip" to purchase Africans to work on their sugar plantation in Cuba? The answer to these questions can be found in Pieh's Poro Society training and the fact that his captors took for granted that they had effectively crushed any thought of rebellion out of the enslaved Africans. His early training in Sierra Leone afforded him an advantage over those who had captured him. He had been schooled in understanding the world around him, including the importance of knowing the laws and customs of other peoples.

His captors, on the other hand, assumed that the grueling journey from Africa aboard the *Iesora,* and the seasoning that took place in Cuba, would have broken his will enough that he would submit to whatever they meted out to him. They were hoping for strong but passive "slaves" when they purchased the Africans in June 1839, and they dismissed the possibility that the Africans could *rethink* their enslavement and escape to freedom.

It is the same way today. Black boys can be raised to have a remarkable sense of who they are and what their place is in the world. They can be educated to understand what the world expects of them and how they can change the negative opinions held by educators, law enforcement officials, and policy makers; they can create effective strategies for change in their communities. A summary of these strategies is outlined below:

I. Child–Rearing Strategies of Black Parents

Method	Description	Strategy	Results
White Way	Traditional way of raising black boys. Parallels the way of raising white boys.	Sees institutions as impartial in their delivery of services to black boys. Attempts to get black boys to adjust to the system.	Children run into conflict with institution. Parents or teachers see them as troublemakers and encourage system submission.

Method	Description	Strategy	Results
Gray Way	Challenges institutions regarding treatment of black boys.	Views institutions objectively and is willing to advocate on behalf of black boys. Heavy involvement with institutions through which black boys pass. Willingness to challenge bureaucracies. Organizes other parents and teachers.	Experiences conflict with bureaucracies. Children and adults feel more empowered regarding their ability to change systems.
Black Way	Sees systems as inherently out of touch with black boys' life goals.	While protest is part of strategy, it is a means to an end. Teaches African-centered principles to boys.	Creation of institutions that are responsive to needs of children. Healthy black boys.

II. The Ten Commitments to Raising Black Boys

1. Maintain a strong commitment to educating black boys.

2. Possess a deep and abiding knowledge of global black history.

3. Read at least thirty minutes a day on African/African-American culture and life.

4. Be comfortable in predominantly black environments.

5. Attend African-centered religious institutions.

6. Volunteer at least five hours a month in human service activity that engages black boys.

7. Understand all bureaucracies that impact black boys.

8. Organize against environments oppressive of black boys.

9. Read the following five books:

   Beloved by Toni Morrison
   Yurugu by Marimba Ani
   The Miseducation of the Negro by Carter G. Woodson
   There Is a River by Vincent Harding
   The Art of War by Sun Tzu

10. Teach at least two other persons each month about the Ten Commitments.

III. The "Four Cs" for Raising Black Boys

Consciousness: Begin at young ages to read out loud to boys about heroes and sheroes among African Americans.

• Insist that school systems recognize various cultural holidays that are relevant to Africans in the *Maafa*.

• Provide a broad listening repertoire to black boys that includes jazz, reggae, rhythm and blues, gospel, funk, symphonic works by black composers, rap and soul.

• Take opportunities to visit museums, library exhibits, and other community activities that present black history.

• Encourage black houses of worship to supplement your boy's education by having at least three hours of classes per week devoted to the study of black history.

• Provide educational films that teach the history of Africa, the period of enslavement, and its aftermath.

• Expand images beyond the famine, war, and disaster that characterize coverage of the continent by news organizations.

• Encourage the wearing of African clothing at young ages.

Commitment: Be willing to intervene on behalf of black boys at any level to enhance their life chances.

• Make volunteering with black boys for five hours a month an initiation rite for all members of black social organizations.

Cooperation: Establish more "Mother's Day/Evening Out" programs at African-American churches so that single parents can get relief from parenting.

• Use Title VI of the 1964 Civil Rights Act to ensure the equitable distribution of federal dollars for local projects.

• Encourage adoption among black houses of worship.

• Create reading groups sponsored by black male civic and religious groups that support black boys' reading about African-American culture and life.

Community: Monitor and attend school board meetings in school districts.

• Create political action committees (PACs) that serve the special interests of the black community.

• Target for selective buying businesses that have a history of harassing and underemploying African Americans, particularly boys.

• Systematically write congressional representatives to make sure they are responsive to legislation that affects the lives of black children.

• Create booster clubs that enourage the purchase of computer technology for black children.

• Organize groups of African-American houses of worship to build educational facilities to meet the needs of black children.

• Encourage black houses of worship to create credit unions for the communities they serve.

• Where possible, place money in African-American-owned banks.

• Sponsor summer-abroad study programs in Africa.

IV. Birthing Circles

▸ Designating a person to monitor the mother's prenatal care, i.e., making sure that appointments are kept and accompanying her to doctor visits during the pregnancy

▸ Designating a person (male or female) to join the mother for prenatal Lamaze, nutrition, or exercise classes

► Designating a person to serve as a backup for completing the paperwork associated with childbirth

► Designating a person to serve as an information specialist on such things as naming, postbirth ceremonies, and health information

► Designating a person to accompany the mother into the delivery room

V. Young Warriors Councils

The fifth year should include the following activities:

► Members of the Young Warriors Council and the seven Young Warriors should hold monthly meetings.

► Each of the seven Young Warriors should read three age-appropriate books during the first year.

► The newly formed Young Warriors Council should take field trips, discuss healthy living, and provide science instruction and lectures that teach the boys about African history and culture.

► At the end of twelve months, the Young Warriors Council should conduct an agreed-upon ceremony that inducts the boys into their sixth year.

► The sixth year should repeat the basic curriculum of the fifth year, adding information technology as a key component of the learning process.

► The seventh year begins the study of law and media.

► The seventh and eighth years should expand on what the Young Warriors have already learned, particularly in the areas of media and law.

► The ninth and tenth years are critical in the development of

Young Warriors, and the councils should be very vigilant in monitoring the institutions that are instructing their boys.

▶ The eleventh and twelfth years are looking-ahead years for the rites-of-passage ceremony, celebrating the Seven Warriors turning thirteen.

These checklists summarize the central methods for raising healthy black boys in America. They should be adapted to the needs of the local communities in which they will be implemented, and serve as guidelines for the persons in charge of the Young Warriors Councils.

9

Epilogue

Parable of the White Elephant

All African Americans and well-meaning nonblack people in America should be outraged at what has happened and continues to happen to black boys and men in this country. When they hear about Diallo, Byrd, the high incarceration rates of black males, drugs and the CIA connection, low levels of academic performance by young black males, and so on, there should be a cry for retribution and change from those who claim to want the best for black boys and men.

Instead, what is found is a free-floating frustration toward black males by people tired of hearing their "excuses." Books, articles, and television programs woefully lament the "vanishing black family" abandoned by the black male who has been proclaimed, like some animal, to be "an endangered species." Many black women discuss the shortage of "good" black men and wistfully talk of the importance of being "flexible" in securing companionship, which often means going beyond traditionally constructed racial and gender boundaries. Rarely do any of these "analyses" factor in racism as related ostensibly to nearly every condition facing black men. Racism and its not-so-subtle perpetrators such as popular radio talk-show hosts and presidential candidates have been extraordinarily successful in making it unpopular to attribute anything negative associated with black males to skin color. Explanations in these directions are cast as an attempt to "play the race card." Discrimination's mutable presence has lulled black males and others into thinking that whatever happens to them is completely their fault and that they need to "quit blaming the white man" for their fate.

Imagine you own a family compound you built from the ground up. It is neat, clean, well ventilated, and has all the accoutrements that you need to live. Your extended family lives in the compound, and you enjoy their presence each day when you return from work. Cooperative management of the compound based on ancient values makes it an Eden-like place.

One day you come home to find a large white elephant wreaking havoc inside the compound. It is trampling over everything you built, defecating on the walkways, uprooting the elaborate shrubbery that took years to plant and prune, destroying everything in sight.

You straighten things out as best you can, but the elephant continues its rampage. It ignores your pleas to leave. In fact, it attempts to trample you. You continue to repair, clean, and rebuild the home, but the white elephant continues to come periodically, hell-bent on its mission of destruction. You organize your relatives to ward off the beast, but the elephant continues to destroy, despite your collective efforts to fend it off. Debates ensue within the family about the best way to destroy the animal; it has killed members of the family that the compound was designed to nurture and protect.

A decision is made by desperate family members to ignore the beast and instead focus on the animal's destruction. Eventually, you devote all of your energy to cleaning up and replacing the things the animal has destroyed.

You actually begin to ignore the elephant and adjust to its destructive behavior. Family members continue to be lost, but little attention is devoted to understanding the wild elephant. All of your energy is focused on cleaning and repairing the damage wrought by the beast. You encourage your family members to do the same.

Other compounds in the neighborhood have had similar visits by white elephants, and you tell your friends to ignore them, to focus instead on the damage the elephants cause.

Eventually, you die, but your message has penetrated the minds of your descendants: they believe the white elephant, still on a rampage after many years, is only a secondary problem, and so they, too, focus on cleaning materials, wood, bricks, and mortar, to try to rebuild after the rampaging white beast metes out its destruction. An entire culture and literature evolves around repairing furniture, building more sturdy walls, painting and redecorating, while the elephant continues to destroy. The elephant itself is all but forgotten by members of your family and the neighboring compounds.

Like the white elephant, racism's influence on everyday behavior among both blacks and whites has become so acceptable that we rarely even see the beast, though it may stand directly in front of us. Members of the black community may advise that we ignore the white elephant, and may actually blame its victims for the destruction in their lives. Racism is so inherent and accepted that even talking about it as a primary reason for explaining the conditions of African-American males is ridiculed. "The end of racism" as D'Souza calls it, though wished for, is not practiced. Cinque's sons are still left without a father to guide them, theories to understand them, and institutions to support them.

Though Joseph Cinque returned to Africa, he never really went home. His two years in captivity had taken a toll on his village and family. Speculations to this day abound over what happened to him. Some say he went to Jamaica (rumors persist that he is buried there) and began to dabble in the same slavery that had taken him from his family. This gossip, provided mostly by members of the American Missionary Association, whose officials were miffed at Cinque's rejection of Christianity after they had been instrumental in his defense, attempted to discredit him and to reinforce the notion that you could take the "heathen" out of the "jungle" but that the "jungle" would remain within the "heathen."

Other rumors had him staying in Sierra Leone, only to die at the doorsteps of the AMA after a long illness. His great-grandson Samuel Hingha Pieh, who has blessed me with his foreword to *The Warrior Method*, believes this is the most likely scenario because it fits with eyewitness reports of his rebuilding his life as much as he could in his native Mende land. Though he never found his wife or his two daughters, he was reunited with his son, Kolima. They worked together in Christian missionary work until Sengbeh's death in 1879.

I have always wondered what happened to Sengbeh Pieh's immediate children. Surely, they wept at their father's captivity. What did they think as they watched their mother beaten and their father dragged off on that dusty Mende road? What did she tell them once the dust had settled? Did they go after their father? Were they captured also? If they were, did they go to Jamaica or Brazil? Did they die a peaceful death in Sierra Leone? Did his grandchildren immigrate to America, and if they did, from what country? Are his descendants in New York? Sao Paulo? Kingston? Chicago? Los Angeles? London? Perhaps they were brought to America and lived just a few hundred miles from where their father was captured and eventually tried.

The period of enslavement continues to bring confusion and paradoxes to Africans in America and throughout the *Maafa*. Cinque's children's children's children could be in school with your son or daughter. They might work next to you. They may be in a managerial suite at a Fortune 500 company, or they may be victims of the drug culture financed by the Central Intelligence Agency during the 1980s in Los Angeles. Cinque's sons are found in the faces of all black men who took the nails from the *Amistad* and made them keys to their freedom.

In February 2000, four police officers were acquitted of killing a young African immigrant named Amadou Diallo. His life was snuffed out in a hail of forty-one 9mm bullets, with nineteen piercing his flesh, including the soles of his feet, as he lay dead in the vestibule of his Bronx apartment. I am angry when I know that the lives of my black brothers and sons are only a thread's width away from a similar fate. I am more concerned now than I was yesterday about white police who stop me, and I will endure the criticism from my nineteen-year-old son who says that I am "overprotective" of him when he goes out with his peers or his girlfriend. Diallo is dead, but his killers walk free; this sends the not-so-subtle message that a black man's life means little. Why do blacks have to convince America that the lives of black men are just as valuable as those of white men? Why do we accept it as so? As Ella Baker put it, "We who believe in freedom will not rest until the killing of black men, black mothers' sons, is as important as the killing of white men, white mothers' sons."

Perhaps Cinque would not be so surprised about how his own captivity and humiliation are reenacted in the everyday harassment of black men who drive, walk, and breathe while being black. Like Cinque, they can all too quickly become captives of a legal system that makes being a black man suspect. Police harass black boys at play and at work much the way they did during enslavement, when black boys were watched, manacled, carded, and pulled over by white men who were anxious about their presence.

Cinque's sons are a metaphor for black men today. Too many of us have been exiled in America for such a long time that our black souls have only a partial understanding of our origins. When our ancestors were forced through the "doors of no return" on the west coast of Africa, never to see their homeland again, much was retained, but more was lost. Our skills as blacksmiths, farmers, bankers, musicians, artists, and physicians honed in various Poro Societies were retained. We used our skills during our enslavement to build the economies of the Western world. What was eventually lost was the history of the various people crammed aboard the slave ships that scattered us throughout the world. So many black men have lost the sense of who we *were* that today it is difficult for us to know who we *are*. The gap between what we know now and what we were in West Africa can be closed by *going back* through the "doors of no return" psychologically, culturally, and, in some cases, physically to rediscover what was left in our ancestral homeland. There is nothing radical about this. White Americans do it when they encourage the presidents of the United States to reconnect with their Irish ancestry. Mexican Americans do it with Cinco de Mayo festivals. The Irish Americans do it with St. Patrick's Day. Passover revisits the spiritual and cultural roots of Judaism. Reconnecting with one's ancestral roots is not only common among American ethnic groups, it is institutionalized in various celebrations and holidays.

On several trips to Africa, I have been overcome with emotion in the men's dungeons at the Castles of Ghana, part of the stone structures that dot the west coast of Africa that held millions of my African ancestors captive as they waited to be shipped like cargo around the world. A systematic and deliberate psychological and physical torture was practiced on the captives in an attempt to poison their positive images of Africa. But Africa persists in the music, art, science, and bodies of those black men captured on the shores of West Africa. It is felt in street drumming, seen in Savion Glover's tap dancing, heard in the lyrics of Dead Prez's raps, seen in Denzel Washington's acting, tasted in Carver's peanut butter, translated in Coltrane's music, and admired in Iverson's moves to the hoop.

Black men in America have their ancestral roots on a continent so very far removed from the consciousness of the vast majority of black males in the *Maafa*. This is not accidental. The removal of African culture from the minds of Africa was systematic and took place over centuries; it continues with the negative images of the continent portrayed by the media. I know that far too many African minds in America are distorted by European values that so permeate their lives that it seems difficult to see what good West African values can do for us today. Images of Africa are emblazoned on media that show swollen bellies, floods, famine, and war. If only Kosovo, Northern Ireland, and Chechnya were shown on CNN, revulsion toward Europe would match that which has been created after centuries of negative portrayals of Africa. Black boys in America are increasingly estranged from their African roots and are given names that reflect this alienation because they teach us nothing about our-selves. Italian names such as Antonio, English names such as William, French names like Leroy are but one small indication of how far from Africa black boys begin their lives. Commonly absent as they grow from childhood to adulthood are the Four Cs—commitment, consciousness, community, and coopera-tion—the essential ingredients for their survival in a society that encourages their destruction.

Like other holding stations on the west coast of Africa, the Castles of Ghana in El Mina and Cape Coast contain openings known as the "doors of no return," the final exit to the ships where black bodies were stacked for transport to various parts of the imperialized white world. Parents, educators, and others who wish to raise, teach, and understand black boys in America must go from ship to shore through these doors to Africa, both physically and psychologically. Like the mythical *Sankofa* bird of Ghana, whose head is tucked under its wing and looks back-ward, they must return to a mind-set when black men knew who they were, what their place was in the world, and what expectations were put upon them. It will be a difficult journey, but it must be made if Cinque's sons are to survive in America. Enough studies have been made, conferences held, and theories offered about the "problem" of black boys in America. It is time to reopen the "doors of no return" to discover what was left in Africa, and shape it to fit the needs of black boys for their past, present, and future.

Appendix A:
Annotated Bibliography

Ani, Marimba. 1994. *Yurugu: An African-Centered Critique of European Cultural Thought and Behavior.* Trenton, N.J.: Africa World Press.

Perhaps the most comprehensive African-centered critique of European systems of thought ever written. The extraordinary breadth of Ani's book provides a starting point for understanding how various European philosophies undergird white supremacist systems. One hundred years from now, this book will be cited, along with Du Bois's *Souls of Black Folk* and Ellison's *Invisible Man*, as one of the great works that analyze the condition of Africans throughout the *Maafa*.

Armah, Ayi Kwei. 1979. *Two Thousand Seasons.* Chicago: Third World Press.

The question is constantly asked, "Why are black folk in the shape they are in?" Armah provides a disturbing answer through a searing novel. He forces the reader to examine the complicity of white supremacy in the condition of African people.

Asante, Molefi, and Abu S. Abarry. 1996. *African Intellectual Heritage.* Philadelphia: Temple University Press.

If you needed one book that provides the vast intellectual scope of African people, this is it. Beginning at 2150 B.C.E. and ending with the Million Man March, Asante and Abarry present the readings and speeches of African people. A basic book for any library serving African people.

Asante, Molefi. 1988. *Afrocentricity.* Trenton, N.J.: Africa World Press.
A book that describes what is now accepted as one of the most important worldviews of the twentieth century.

Asante, Molefi, and Mark Mattson. 1991. *Historical and Cultural Atlas of African Americans.* New York: Macmillan Publishing Co.
This book provides a panoramic view of the history of African Americans—from Egypt to Harlem. It also provides a wealth of photographs, drawings, and maps that help to locate African people geographically, historically, and psychologically. A basic book for understanding African people.

Asante, Molefi. 1993. *Malcolm X as Cultural Hero and Other Afrocentric Essays.* Trenton, N.J.: Africa World Press.
Asante gets specific about issues confronting Africans in the Diaspora, ranging from the image of Malcolm X to violence among Africans.

Barboza, Steven. 1993. *American Jihad: Islam After Malcolm X.* New York: Doubleday.
Barboza explores the varieties of the fastest-growing religion in America. His interviews with Muslims from all walks of life provide an unprecedented view of Islam.

Bell, Derrick. 1992. *Faces at the Bottom of the Well: The Permanence of Racism.* Basic Books.
A life-changing book. The former Harvard professor provides a grim scenario of why African Americans will never achieve equality in this country. A pessimistic yet very realistic book about racism.

Bernal, Martin. 1987, 1991. *Black Athena,* Vols. I and II. New Brunswick, N.J.: Rutgers University Press.

The sheer audacity of Bernal's thesis—that what we call "Greek civilization" is essentially Egyptian—makes these volumes "heavy" reading. The scholarship is unquestionable in Bernal's pursuit of the true root of what is commonly called "Western civilization."

Bowen, W. G., and Derek Bok. 1998. *The Shape of the River.* Princeton: Princeton University Press.

The former presidents of Princeton and Harvard Universities provide the most compelling arguments on why affirmative action works. By giving the reader empirical evidence of affirmative action's positive results, the book destroys common myths: that affirmative action displaces whites, or is a handout. A must-read for anyone who wishes to avoid the hype on affirmative action.

Boyd, Herb, and Robert Allen, eds. 1995. *Brotherman: The Odyssey of Black Men in America.* New York: One World/Ballantine.

One of the best compilations of writings and images of black men. The writers show the infinite and intimate aspects of being a black male in America.

Bradley, Michael. 1978. *The Iceman Inheritance.* New York: Kayode Publications.

Bradley offers the controversial thesis that European racism is evolutionary and biological. Bradley supports this theory with numerous references and forces the reader to examine the possible origins of white supremacy.

Chideya, Farai. 1995. *Don't Believe the Hype: Fighting Cultural Misinformation About African-Americans.* New York: Penguin Books.

The sheer volume of misinformation about African Americans is a primary contributor to rumors of inferiority. Chideya's small but very informative volume presents an array of *facts* that may even surprise those who *think* they know dearly held "truths" about African Americans. A useful handbook for combating racist stereotypes.

Comaroff, Jean, and John Comaroff. 1991. *Of Revelation and Revolution: Christianity, Colonialism and Consciousness in South Africa.* Chicago: University of Chicago Press.

Presents the argument of how Western Christianity was the fundamental rationale for the establishment of apartheid in South Africa.

Diop, Cheikh Anta. 1974. *The African Origin of Civilization.* Westport, Conn.: Lawrence Hill Publishers.

The African genius who first cited anthropological evidence that the Egyptians were black people. A scholarly book that will change your view of Africa.

Du Bois, W.E.B. 1903. *The Souls of Black Folk.* Available in a variety of editions from a variety of publishers.

"The problem of the twentieth century will be the problem of the color line." Du Bois's prophetic words echo even louder as we begin a new millennium and the color problem is still unresolved. If you have not read this book, you have no foundation for understanding anything relative to Africans in America.

Floyd, Samuel. 1995. *The Power of Black Music.* New York: Oxford University Press.

The director of the Center for Black Music Research at Columbia College in Chicago connects all of the dots in the history of African-American music back to its roots in Africa.

Franklin, John Hope. 1989. *Race and History: Selected Essays, 1938–1988.* Baton Rouge: Louisiana State University Press.

A collection of important essays by one of America's leading historians. The sheer sweep of his writing opens new vistas on the struggle of African Americans, and excites the reader to further research.

Fuller, Neely. 1980. *The United Independent Compensatory Code/System/Concept: A Textbook/Workbook for Thought, Speech and/or Action for Victims of Racism (White Supremacy).* Self-published.

Should be read by anyone who truly wishes to understand the nature of white supremacy and its global impact on people of color.

Neely Fuller's self-published book, available at black bookstores around the country, has been a best-seller for years among those who wish to deconstruct the subtleties of white supremacy. An invaluable resource.

Gould, Stephen. 1981. *The Mismeasure of Man.* New York: W.W. Norton.

Gould analyzes the rampant nineteenth-century white supremacy that plagued all of the social and natural sciences. Provides good insight into the fallacies of Western science.

Griaule, Marcel, and Germaine Dieterlen. 1965. *The Pale Fox.* Arizona: The Continuum Foundation.

The classic French anthropological study of the Dogon people of Mali provides a context for understanding indigenous West African religion. The study leaves no doubt about the harmony between science and religion in the Dogon cosmology.

Grimshaw, Anna. 1992. *The C.L.R. James Reader.* London: Blackwell Press.

Some have called the late C.L.R. James the "Socrates" of Africans in the *Maafa*. This would probably be an insult to James, since most consider him far wiser than the Greek with whom he is compared.

Harding, Sandra. 1993. *The "Racial" Economy of Science: Toward a Democratic Future.* Indiana: Indiana University Press.

Critics of Afrocentricity argue that the "natural" sciences are immune to criticisms of racism and androcentricity. Harding's selection of readings proves that, if anything, the so-called "natural" sciences are deeply imbedded with racist ideology that advocates the exploitation of first-world persons.

Harding, Vincent. 1983. *There Is a River: The Black Struggle for Freedom in America.* New York: Vintage Books.

Simply the best history of Africans in America ever written. Harding takes the reader from Africa to the Civil War from the point of view of being African in America. It is a work of sheer beauty.

Holloway, Joseph E. 1990. *Africanisms in American Culture.* Indiana: Indiana University Press.

This book examines the sometimes unnoticed influence that African culture had on the development of American linguistic formation, games, holidays, and food.

Holloway, Joseph E., and Winifred K. Vass. 1993. *The African American Heritage of American English.* Indiana: Indiana University Press.

Holloway and Vass give remarkable examples of the debt owed to the linguistic contributions of Africans in America. Place names as well as maps are provided to show how influential Africans were in naming many locations throughout the United States.

Karenga, Maulana. 1993. *Introduction to Black Studies.* Los Angeles, Calif.: Kawaida Publications.

No other book presents as much information in so few pages as Karenga's book. The creator of Kwanzaa, this book provides a basic outline on how Black Studies should be approached.

Lewis, David Levering. 1993. *W.E.B. Du Bois: Biography of a Race.* New York: Henry Holt and Co.

Du Bois's life, spanning nearly a century, is the story of blacks in the twentieth century. The author brilliantly details his genius and commitment to fighting racism. One cannot understand race in the twentieth century unless one understands the life of Du Bois.

Lipschutz, Mark R., and R. Kent Rasmussen. 1986. *Dictionary of African Historical Biography.* Berkeley, Calif.: University of California Press.

An essential reference book for understanding "who's who" in Africa. Covers political, literary, and historical figures on the African continent.

Madhubuti, Haki. 1980. *Black Men: Obsolete, Single, Dangerous?* Chicago: Third World Press.

The chapter on the books that all Africans need to read is worth the purchase itself. Madhubuti addresses a range of issues involving African men. A must for every library.

Mbiti, John S. 1975. *Introduction to African Religions.* London: Heinemann Press.
A fundamental book for understanding African religions. Mbiti also examines the influence of Christianity, Islam, and other religions on Africa, and how African religions have influenced so-called Western religions.

Morrison, Toni. 1992. *Playing in the Dark: Whiteness and the Literary Imagination.* Cambridge, Mass.: Harvard University Press.
The importance of this book in understanding how Hawthorne, Melville, Twain, and other literary figures used Africans in developing American literature cannot be overstated. Morrison's analysis of a new literary criticism based on understanding the "Africanization" of American literature is flawless and extraordinary.

Morrison, Toni. 1987. *Beloved.* New York: Alfred A. Knopf.
The greatest African-American love story ever told. Those who read it and don't understand it miss the emotional impact of slavery on Africans in America. Read it again and again.

Pieterse, Jan Nederven. 1992. *White on Black: Images of Africa and Blacks in Western Popular Culture.* New Haven, Conn.: Yale University Press.
A rare book that documents, through extensive photographs and graphics, how white supremacy was (is) interwoven throughout the history of European domination of the earth. The Dutch author's indictment of the cultural supports of white supremacy is rare among European social scientists.

Rowan, Carl. 1996. *The Coming Race War in America.* New York: Little, Brown and Company.
A surprising yet provocative book written by one of the world's leading black journalists. Rowan outlines a chilling scenario of race

relations in the world that pulls together a series of facts alone that makes the book worthwhile reading.

Saxton, Alexander. 1990. *The Rise and Fall of the White Republic*. London: Verso Press.

Saxton offers the hypothesis that the Americanization of nineteenth-century America was in actuality the conscious and deliberate attempt to structure a "white republic" that viewed all persons of color—Asians, Africans, and American Indians—as inferior.

Sertima, Ivan Van. 1987, 1988. *African Presence in Early Europe and Asia*. New Brunswick, N.J.: Transaction Publishers.

Van Sertima traces early explorations into Europe and Asia by Africans. These works leave the reader with a broader understanding of how Africa has influenced the rest of the world.

Welsing, Frances Cress. 1991. *The Isis Papers*. Chicago: Third World Press.

The number-one-selling nonfiction book among African Americans from 1991 to 1993. Welsing's thesis on the global system of white supremacy is still unchallenged. A most important book to read.

Williams, Chancellor. 1976. *The Destruction of Black Civilization*. Chicago: Third World Press.

One of the most important books on why black civilizations declined from their former glory. Unsparing in his critique of those who raped the African continent, Williams seeks to understand the present through a deeper understanding of the past.

Woodson, Carter G. 1990. *The Miseducation of the Negro*. Nashville, Tenn.: Winston-Derek Publishers.

The classic book offered by the "father" of African-American history, on why blacks *and* whites have been miseducated.

Appendix B
Annotated Bibliography of Books for Black Children

Grades 1–6

Verna, Aardema. 1975. *Why Mosquitoes Buzz in People's Ear.* New York: Dial.

A circular tale that will make children think about why things are the way they are. Based on an African folktale, the story is timeless.

Aesop's Fables. Available in a variety of editions from a variety of publishers.

The stories of animals that have thrilled children of all colors for ages. They are the basis of the Anansi stories of the Caribbean and the Uncle Remus stories of the United States.

Hamilton, Virginia. 1987. *The People Could Fly.* New York: Alfred A. Knopf.

Hamilton's collection of folktales is one of the best ever compiled. The stories are universal and base much of their content on African legends about freedom and restoration.

Steptoe, John. 1987. *Mufaro's Beautiful Daughters: An African Tale.* New York: Lothrop, Lee & Shepard.

This book is a good example of how well-told stories of Africa can replace the European fairy tale. In this case, it's Cinderella, but with a beautiful twist.

Walker, Alice. 1991. *Finding the Green Stone.* New York: Harcourt Brace.

Alice Walker's joyous tale of Katie and Johnny's search for a mysterious green stone. The tale tells a wonderful story of generosity, regret, and strength by one of America's favorite authors.

Wague, Diakite Baba. 1997. *The Hunterman and the Crocodile: A West African Folktale.* New York: Scholastic Trade.

The Malian author weaves and intriguing tale of Bamba the Crocodile and Donso the Hunterman. The author tells a wonderful story of reconciliation. The illustrations themselves are fascinating.

Grades 7–12

Dumas, Alexander. 1996. *The Count of Monte Cristo.* New York: Modern Library.

The timeless tale written by Dumas opens a world of intrigue and revenge by the black author. The issue of injustice can be a strong point of discussion to those who read the novel.

Hansberry, Lorraine. Reprint, 1994. *A Raisin in the Sun.* New York: Vintage Classics.

The fast-paced story of the effects of racism on a Chicago family. Struggling with the death of their father, the children represent the hopes and aspirations of African Americans during the civil rights era.

Hurston, Zora Neale. 1937. *Their Eyes Were Watching God.* New York: J. B. Lippincott Co.

A book that helps men understand the voice of black women and the oppression they encounter at the hands of men.

Malcolm X. Reissue edition (December 1989). *The Autobiography of Malcolm X.* New York: African American Images. *Autobiography* by W.E.B. Du Bois, *Up from Slavery* by Booker T. Washington, and Malcolm's life are called by some the greatest autobiographies of African-American men. The book, written during the 1960s, is timeless in the challenges faced by African-American men. It will transform anyone who reads it.

Wright, Richard. 1998. *Black Boy.* New York: Harper Perennial Library.
    One of the greatest autobiographies of all time. Wright tells a period story that is amazingly relevant for today's black boys. A classic narrative that gives black boys an unedited view of segregation in the South.

Index

Abdul-Jabbar, Kareem, 182
Abu-Jamal, Mumia, 125
academic performance, 116–21
Adams, John Quincy, xxv–xxvi
adolescence, 147–77
  black rage and, 156–60
  derivation and definition of,
    147–48
  educational issues in, 168–69
  health issues in, 160–62
  male-female relationships in, 152–56,
    170–77
  rites-of-passage ceremonies in, 144,
    150–52
  violence in, 149–50
  Warriors Councils in, 162–68
  work in, 169–70
adoption, 92–93
Aetna Life, 171
Afraid of the Dark (Myers), 159–60
Africa, 21–22, 71, 137, 144
  education about, 78–79
  summer-abroad study programs in,
    100–101
Africana (Gates and Appiah), 71
African clothing, 80, 88
Akbar, Na'im, 73

alcohol, 135, 150, 161
Ali, Muhammad, 22
alien-self disorders, 73
Alinsky, Saul, 62
Alvarado, Manuel, 122
American Indians, 149, 150, 162
American Missionary Association
  (AMA), xxvii, xxviii, 203
American Tragedy, 28
Amistad (movie), 130
Amistad (ship), xviii–xxi, xxii, 3, 167, 192,
  204
Angelou, Maya, 5
Ani, Marimba, 61, 70, 195
anti-self disorders, 73
Antonio (*Amistad* cabin boy), xviii
apartheid, 33
*Appeal to the Colored Citizens of the
  World* (Walker), 57
Appiah, Anthony, 71
Armah, Ayi Kwei, 80–81, 173
Art of War, The (Sun Tzu), 61, 195
Asante, Molefi, 70
Asian Americans, 149
asthma, 74
Attention Deficit Disorder, 45–46
Atwater, Lee, 29–30

Baby and Child Care (Spock), 44
Back to Africa movement, 21, 58
Baker, Ella, 172, 205
banks, black-owned, 99
bar mitzvah ceremonies, 150–51, 162
Baseline Essays, 70
Bean, Robert Bennett, 36
Before the Mayflower (Bennett), 141
Belafonte, Harry, 38
Bell, Derrick, 43, 158
Bell Curve, The (Murray and
   Herrnstein), 12
Beloved (Morrison), 61, 173, 189–91,
   195
Beloved (movie), 188
Bettelheim, Bruno, 76
"Beyond the Nationalism of Fools"
   (Rivers), 34–35
Biko, Steven, 200
birth defects, 105–6
Birthing Circles, 106–9, 110–11, 124,
   130, 131–32, 133, 134, 135, 164,
   182, 197–98
Birth of a Nation, The, 26, 31–32, 38
Black Child, The (Laye), 147
black cultural holidays, 76
blackface, 38
black females, 151
   Birthing Circles and, 106–9, 110–11,
      124, 131–32, 197–98
   relationship between black males and,
      13, 14, 50–51, 80–81, 88–91,
      152–56, 170–77, 184–91
black history, 56–57, 78
Black History Month, 55, 64, 76, 79,
   130
*Black Macho and the Myth of the
   Superwoman* (Wallace), 171
black males
   constructive behavior patterns of,
      9–12
   criminal justice system and, 5–6
   criticism among, 182–84
   effects of adaptation on, 38–40
   handguns and, 121–22
   images of, 23–40
   puberty and, 119
   raising of, 41–62
   relationship between black females
      and, 13, 14, 50–51, 80–81, 88–91,
      152–56, 170–77, 184–91
   as role models, 182–84

self-destructive behavior of, 7–9,
   11–12, 39–40, 74
self-hatred of, 39–40
sexuality of, 27–34, 119–21
suicide and, 39–40
black males, by age group
   from conception to four, 102–11
   from 5 to 12, 112–46
   from 13 to 21, 147–77
   from 22 through homegoing, 178–91
Black Men (Madhubuti), 141
black rage, 156–60
Black Rage (Grier and Cobbs), 156–57
Black Way, of child rearing, 44, 50–53,
   93, 194
Bob Jones University, 31
Botha, P. W., 34
boycotts, 97
Boys Clubs, 60, 130
Boy Scouts of America, 130, 148
Boyz in the Hood, 91
Bradley, Bill, 182
Brewer, Rose, 90–91
Brooks, Henri, 95
Brown, Claude, 155
Brown, John, 55
Brown, Thomas, 176
Brown v. Board of Education, 38–39, 70,
   86–87
Bryant, Carolyn and Roy, 175
bureaucracies, 60
burial grounds, 143
Bush, George, 29
busing riots, 87
Butler, Niki, 145
Byrd, James, Jr., 176–77

Calderon de la Barca, A., xxiii–xxiv
Cantor, George, 142
Carew family, 3
Carmichael, Stokely, 22
Carnegie Council on Adolescent
   Development, 121
Carver, George Washington, 28, 94, 206
Castles of Ghana, xvii, 206, 207
Celestino (*Amistad* cook), xviii, xix–xx
Centers for Disease Control and
   Prevention (CDC), 121, 128–29
Central Intelligence Agency (CIA), 200,
   204
Césaire, Aimé, 58
charter schools, 94

Childhood and Society (Erikson), 157
child rearing, 44–53, 193–94
    Black Way of, 44, 50–53, 93, 194
    Gray Way of, 44, 49–50, 93, 194
    Warrior Method of, 53–62, 93, 195
    White Way of, 44, 45–48, 94, 170, 193
Chuck D, 28
Cinque, Joseph (Sengbeh Pieh), 2, 9, 13,
        15, 111, 130, 137, 167, 181, 192–93
    Amistad voyage of, xviii–xxi
    capture of, xv, xvi
    descendants of, 3, 4, 204
    in Middle Passage, xvii–xviii
    rebellion led by, xx–xxi
    in return to Sierra Leone, xxvii–xxviii,
        3–4, 203
    trial of, xxi–xxvi
Civil Rights Act (1964), 95
Civil War, U.S., xxviii, 37
clans, 131–32
Clarke, John Henrik, 70, 94
classical music, 48
Clinton, Hillary, 91
Cobbs, Price, 156–57
colleges and universities, black, xxvii, 7,
        52, 72, 85–86, 141, 168–69
Collins, Marva, 69
Color Purple, The (Walker), 172, 173
Coltrane, John, 48, 206
Columbine massacre, 6
commitment, 56, 72, 81–84, 196
community, 72, 93–101, 151, 197
"Compromise of 1877," 86
computers, 98, 124–26, 144
Congressional Black Caucus, 12
consciousness, 72–81, 196
    African-centered, 57–58, 75–81
    four personality disorders and,
        73–75
    "white," 74–75
Constitution, U.S., 37, 96
cooperation, 72, 85–93, 196–97
"cooperative economics," 99, 133, 144
Cosby, Bill, 182
cotillions, 151
Cotton Club, 38
Covey, James, xxiv
Coward, Raymond, 163
Crenshaw, Geneva, 44
Criminal Justice, Criminal Violence
        (Silberman), 158–59
criminal justice system, 5–6, 81–83

Crummell, Alexander, 21
Curry, George, 89

Darwin, Charles, 116
Davis, Angela, 172
Dead Prez, 119, 206
Death Row, 168
Debt, The (Robinson), 170–71
Delany, Martin, 57
Democratic Party, 96
Diallo, Amadou, 125, 200, 204–5
"digital gap," 98, 123, 125–26
Doby, Larry, 180
Drew, Charles, 124
drugs, 150, 161–62
D'Souza, Dinesh, 70, 203
DuBois, W. E. B., 21, 22, 48, 58, 75, 86,
        169
Dukakis, Michael, 29
Duke, David, 55
Dumas, Leon, 58

Ebert, Roger, 32
education, 46–47, 48, 83–84, 94, 168–69
    for black students, 63–72
    commitment to, 56
    cooperation and, 85–87
    performance statistics in, 116–21
Eisenhower, Dwight D., 72
elections, U.S.
    of 1988, 29–30
    of 2000, 96
emancipation, xxviii
Encyclopaedia Britannica, 37
epistemological racism, 127–28
Erikson, Erik, 157
Even the Rat Was White (Guthrie), 127
eye contact, 7, 38, 155

Faces at the Bottom of the Well (Bell),
        158
families, 88–93, 170, 200–201
Fanon and the Crisis of European Man
        (Gordon), 47
Farrakhan, Louis, 39, 183
fathers, absent, 89
FBI Uniform Crime Statistics, 7
Ferrer, Raymond, xviii, xix, xx
Fifteenth Amendment, 96
financial education, 144–45
Fisk University, xxvii, 7, 72, 86, 169
Forsyth, John, xxiii

48 Hours, 160
Four Cs, 72–101, 166–67, 182, 207
    commitment, 72, 81–84, 196
    community, 72, 93–101, 197
    consciousness, 72–81, 196
    cooperation, 72, 84–93, 196–97
Franklin, John Hope, 37
Frazier, E. Franklin, 8, 151
Fuller, Neely, 172

Garner, Margaret, 61
Garrison, William Lloyd, xxii
Garvey, Marcus, 21, 58
Gates, Bill, 98
Gates, Henry Louis "Skip," 71
Gerbner, George, 122–23
Ghana, xvii, 3, 58, 80, 88, 100, 206, 207
Gibbs, Josiah Willard, xxiv
Gibson, Josh, 180
Gilbert, Rocano, 162
Giovanni, Nikki, 169
Girls Clubs, 60, 130
Glover, Savion, 206
Goodwin, Frederick, 11–12
Gordon, Lewis, 47–48
Grabeau (shipmate of Cinque), xx
Graham, Lawrence Otis, 8
Grandmaster Flash and the Furious
    Five, 118–19
Gray Way, of child rearing, 44, 49–50,
    93, 194
Grier, William, 156–57
Griffith, D. W., 26
griots, 10
Gubar, Susan, 29–30
Gutch, Robin, 122
Guthrie, Robert, 127, 128
Gutman, Herbert, 90

hairstyles, 39
Hale, Matthew, 30
Haley, Alex, 10
Hamer, Fannie Lou, 175
Harding, Vincent, 61, 195
Hare, Nathan, 8, 73
Harlem Renaissance, 58
Hayes, Rutherford B., 86
Healers, 11–12
health care, 110–11
health issues, 121–26, 160–62
Henry, Patrick, 48
Herrnstein, Richard, 12

hip-hop. *See* rap music
Hip Hop Hustlers, 8, 9
Hispanics. *See* Latinos
Historic Landmarks of Black America
    (Cantor), 142
History of the American People (Wilson),
    31
Holocaust, xivn., 78
Homicide in the United States
    (MacKellar and Yanagishita), 149
homicide rates, 5, 7, 9, 39, 121, 149–50
"homisuicidal behavior," 40
hooks, bell, 172
Horton, Willie, 26, 29
Hot Tax war, 4
House of Representatives, U.S., 96, 97
human service activities, 60

I Believe in Myself (IBIM), 124
Iesora, xv, xvii–xviii, xix, 193
Imani, 134
immunization, 160–61
Industrial Revolution, 148
infants, 102–11
    Birthing Circles for, 106–9, 110–11,
        124, 130
    early hurdles for, 110–11
    mortality rates for, 6, 102–3, 104,
        110
    naming of, 109–10
integration, 39, 86–87
Internet, 123, 125, 137, 144
investment clubs, 145

Jackson, Chuck, 76–77
Jackson, Michael, 27, 39
jazz, 48, 86, 140
Jefferson, Thomas, 36, 48, 64
Jemison, Mae, 124
Jews, xvin., 149, 150–51, 162
Jim Crow laws and era, xxviii, 173–74
Jones, Laurence Clifton, 69
Jordan, Michael, 28, 182
Jordan, Vernon, 183
Jordan, Winthrop, 29
Judson, Andrew, xxv
Justice Department, U.S., 5, 6

Kali (shipmate of Cinque), xxvi, xxvii
karamu, 135, 166
Kardiner, Abram, 157
Karenga, Maulana, 72, 133

Kennedy, John F., 21
Kente cloth, 79, 88, 134, 144, 166
Khun Anup, 178
Killers, 9
King, Coretta Scott, 176
King, Martin Luther, Jr., 16, 22, 76, 88,
    130, 142, 169, 175
King, Rodney, 158
King Kong, 31–32
Kujichagulia, 133
Ku Klux Klan, xxviii, 31
Kunjufu, Jawanza, 85, 117
Kuumba, 134
Kwanzaa, 52, 76, 99, 130, 133, 187

Lake Mohonk Conferences, 86
Latimer, Lewis, 124
Latinos, 6, 12, 96, 117, 129, 149, 160
law, study of, 138
Laye, Camara, 147
learning, active vs. passive, 14
Lee, Kurtis, 54
Lefkowitz, Mary, 70
Lemmon, Jack, 28
Levine, Richard, 54
Levitt, Joshua, xxv
libation ceremonies, 132, 143–44,
    164–65
Liddy, G. Gordon, 181
life expectancies, 103–4
Lil' Bow Wow, 139–40
Lincoln, Abraham, 36
Louima, Abner, 125
Lucas, George, 32
lynchings, xxviii, 26, 30–31, 33, 37, 174–77

Maafa, xvin., 57, 72, 75, 76, 88, 132, 137,
    141, 151, 204, 206
McBurnett, Keith, 127
macho behavior, 117, 188
McIntyre, Charshee, 81–82
MacKellar, F. Landis, 149
McMillan, Terry, 171
Madhubuti, Haki, 141, 172
Mailer, Norman, 73
Malcolm X, 16, 39, 76, 156
Malcolm X Academy, 70
malformations, birth, 105–6
Malian storytellers, 10
Mandela, Nelson, 33, 182
Mapplethorpe, Robert, 30
Margai family, 3

Mark of Oppression (Kardiner and
    Ovesey), 157
marriage, interracial, 73
Marsalis, Wynton, 28
Maultsby, Portia, 140
Mayagilalo, xvi
Meade, Richard, xxi
media, study of, 122–23, 138
Meditations from the Pen of Mrs. Maria
    Stewart (Stewart), 57
Mee kema, 4
"mega" black churches, 99
Mende people and language, xv, xvii,
    xxiv, 3–4, 13–15, 167
mental health, 127–29
Mfume, Kweisi, 183
middle class, 8
Middle Passage, xv, xvi–xviii
Milam, J. W., 175
Million Man March, 39, 125, 160
Minoso, Minnie, 180
minstrels, 9
Miseducation of the Negro, The
    (Woodson), 61, 195
Monroe Doctrine, xxi, xxiii
Montez, Pedro, xviii, xix, xx
Moore, Audley, 58
Moreland, Mantan, 38
Morrison, Toni, 61, 173, 189, 195
"Mother's Day/Evening Out" programs,
    92
movies
    black males as portrayed in, 27–28,
        31–33, 38–39, 91, 160
    blacks rescued by whites in, 54–55
    relationships between black men and
        women in, 171–72, 188–89
Moynihan, Daniel Patrick, 90
Muhammad, Elijah, 58
Murphy, Eddie, 160
Murray, Carolyn, 138
Murray, Charles, 12
music, 76–77, 111, 118–19, 124, 139–40
Myers, Jim, 159–60

names, 21, 109–10, 207
National Assessment of Educational
    Performance (NAEP), 116
National Association for the
    Advancement of Colored People
    (NAACP), 123
Nation of Islam, 58

Native Americans, 149, 150, 162
Naylor, Gloria, 172
NBC, 97
Négritude movement, 58
Negro Baseball Leagues, 180
New Color of Success, The (Butler),
    145
Nguzo Saba (Seven Principles), 52,
    133–34
Nia, 133
"nigga," use of term, 65–66, 186
nigrescence, 44
Nike, 97
Nixon's Piano (O'Reilly), 72
Nkrumah, Kwame, 22
Nkrumah family, 3
North, Oliver, 181
Notes on the State of Virginia (Jefferson),
    36
Not Out of Africa (Lefkowitz), 70
Nzingha, Yaa Asantewa, 54

Ocean Hill–Brownsville controversy, 87
100 Black Men, 93
O'Neill, Eugene, 147
oratorical contests, 137
O'Reilly, Kenneth, 72
organic disorders, 74
Origin of the Species (Darwin), 116
Osborne, Jason, 117
Ovesey, Lionel, 157

PACs (political action committees),
    95–97
Parham, Thomas, 44
Parks, Rosa, 2, 20, 175
Patton, Adell, 13
PBS, 71
*Physicians, Colonial Racism, and
    Diaspora in West Africa* (Patton),
    13
Pieh, Kolima, xxvii, 3, 4, 203
Pieh, Peter, 4
Pieh, Samuel Hingha, 1–4, 203
Pieh, Sengbeh. *See* Cinque, Joseph
Pieterse, Jan Nederveen, 29
Piney Woods Country Life School, 69
Pipher, Mary, 12
Plessy v. Ferguson, 86, 94
Poitier, Sidney, 38
police harassment and violence, 43, 45,
    138–39, 188, 204–5

political action committees (PACs),
    96–97
Poro Societies, 9, 13–15, 130, 131–32,
    137, 151, 166, 167, 170, 192,
    205
prisons, in criminal justice system, 5–6,
    81–83
prosperity ministries, 99
proverbs, 41, 85, 112, 200
Public Enemy, 28, 119
Pulp Fiction, 28

"race card," 30
rap music, 38, 77, 118–19, 124, 139–40,
    186
Rasbury, Angel, 141
reading, 67, 69, 92
    annotated bibliography for, 209–16
    on black culture, 58–59, 75–76
    children's books, 217–19
    "must read" titles, 61, 195
    Young Warriors Councils and, 135–36,
        141, 144
Reagan, Ronald, 181
Reconstruction, 86
Reed, Ishmael, 23
Reik, Theodore, 50
religious institutions, African-centered,
    59–60, 77–78, 92–93, 98–99
Reviving Ophelia (Pipher), 12
Rhames, Ving, 27–28
Ritalin, 45–46
rites-of-passage ceremonies, 144,
    150–52, 162–68
Rivers, Eugene, 34–35
Robinson, Jackie, 180
Robinson, Randall, 170–71, 183
Rodman, Dennis, 27, 39
Rodriguez, Max, 141
Roosevelt, Franklin D., 21
Roots (Haley), 10, 173
Rosewood, Fla., 33
Ruiz, Jose, xviii, xix, xx
Ruth, Babe, 180

Sacred Fire (Taylor), 141
St. Patrick's Day, 76, 79, 206
Sande Societies, 13
Scheurich, James, 127
Schlesinger, Arthur, 70–71
school board meetings, 95
school desegregation, 86–87

schools. *See* education
school shootings, 6, 128
Scottsboro Boys, 26, 32
Seminars on African-American
    Relationships (SOAR), 187–88
Senghor, Leopold, 58
Sentencing Project, 5, 149
Seven Principles (*Nguzo Saba*), 52,
    133–34
sexism, 12, 186
sex ratio, 184–85
Shakespeare, William, 33, 147
Shakur, Tupac, 119
Sharpton, Al, 183
Sierra Leone, xv, xxi, xxvii, 3–4, 13–15,
    111, 192, 203
Signorelli, Nancy, 122
Silberman, Charles, 158–59
Simba program, 162
Simpson, O. J., 28, 30
Singleton, John, 91
slave rebellions, xvii, xx–xxi, xxii
slave trade, xv–xvii, 171
Smalls, Biggie, 119
Smith, Benjamin Nathaniel, 31
Snoop Doggy Dogg, 140
SOAR (Seminars on African-American
    Relationships), 187
social organizations, 92
"Some Racial Peculiarities of the Negro
    Brain" (Bean), 36
Souls of Black Folk (DuBois), 75
South Africa, 33–34
Southworth, Michael, 6–7
spelling bees, 137
Spock, Benjamin, 44, 45
*Star Wars Episode I: The Phantom
    Menace,* 32–33
Steele, Claude, 117
sterilization, 128
Stewart, Maria, 57
Strategists, 10
suburban alienation, 6–7
Sue, Stanley, 152
Sun Tzu, 61, 195
Super Slaves, 8, 10, 73, 183
Supreme Court, U.S., xxv, xxvi
Sutton, Katie, 102

Tappan, Lewis, xxii, xxv, xxvii
Taylor, Carol, 141
Taylor, Cheo, 162

"technological gap," 97, 123,
    125–26
television, 122–23, 125, 138
Tennessee State Black Caucus, 95
Terman, Lewis, 128
Terrell, Mary Church, 94
There Is a River (Harding), 61, 195
Thomas, Charles, 119
Thomas, Derrick, 40
Till, Emmett, 26, 33, 78, 175–76
Too Short, 39
Toure, Kwame, 22
Treisman, Urie, 69
Truth, Sojourner, 172
Truth and Reconciliation Commission,
    33–34
Tulsa, Okla., 33
Turner, Mary, 174–75
Turner, Nat, xxii
Tutu, Archbishop Emeritus Desmond,
    33, 182
2 Live Crew, 39
Two Thousand Seasons (Armah), 80–81,
    173

Ujamaa, 99, 133, 144
Ujima, 133, 169
Umoja, 133
United Methodist Church Conference,
    3
United Press International (UPI), 124
universities and colleges, black, xxvii, 7,
    52, 72, 85–86, 141, 168–69

Van Buren, Martin, xxii–xxiii, xxv, xxvii
Vesey, Denmark, 57
violence, 5–9, 39, 121–26, 149–50, 182
    black rage and, 156–60
    police harassment and, 43, 45, 138–39,
        188, 204–5
vouchers, school, 94

Waiting to Exhale (McMillan), 171
Walker, Alice, 172, 173
Walker, David, xxii, 57
Walker, Madame C. J., 39
Wallace, Michele, 171
Walnut Street Jail, 82
Wanna-nevah-bees, 8–9
Warrior Method, of child rearing, 53–62,
    83, 93
    Ten Commitments of, 56–62, 195

Warriors
  description of, 9–10
  necessary tools for, 63–101
Washington, Booker T., 71, 86, 94
Washington, Denzel, 206
Washington, George, 64, 71, 72
Washington, U.S.S., xxi
Wells-Barnett, Ida B., 48, 57
West Africa, 78–79, 100
West Side Preparatory, 69
White on Black (Pieterse), 29
White Over Black (Jordan), 29
White Way, of child rearing, 44, 45–48,
  94, 170, 193
Williams, Bert, 38
Wilson, Woodrow, 31
Winbush, Dorothy, 180
Winbush, Faraji Khalid, 109
Winbush, Harold, 178–81, 188
Winbush, Harold "Windy," 18–20, 22,
  178
Winbush, Myrna, 20
Winbush, Omari Lateef, 109
Winbush, Ron, 16–18, 19, 20, 180

Winbush, Sharifa Hasin, 109
Winter's Tale, The (Shakespeare), 147
Wise, Tim, 55
Wollen, Tana, 122
Women of Brewster Place, The (Naylor),
  172
Wonders of the African World, 71
Woods, Tiger, 28
Woodson, Carter G., 61, 63, 69, 94,
  195
words, remaking of, 66
work, 169–70
World Church of the Creator, 30
Wright, Bobby, 158
Wright, Mose, 175

Yanagishita, Machiko, 149
Young, Michelle, 127
Young Warriors Councils, 130–46, 160,
  182
  adolescence and, 162–68
  induction into, 132–36
  steps in, 131–46, 198–99
Yurugu (Ani), 61, 195